Excuse Me, Sir...
Your Socks are on Fire

Larry Weill

North Country Books, Inc.
Utica, New York

Excuse Me, Sir... Your Socks are on Fire

Copyright © 2005
by Larry Weill

Fourth Printing 2011

ISBN 1-59531-000-2
ISBN-13 978-1-59531-000-2

Library of Congress Cataloging-in-Publication Data

Weill, Larry.
  Excuse me, sir-- your socks are on fire / by Larry Weill.
    p. cm.
  ISBN 1-59531-000-2 (alk. paper)
  1. Weill, Larry. 2. Park rangers--New York (State)--Adirondack
Park--Biography. 3. New York (State). Dept. of Environmental
Conservation--Officials and employees--Biography. 4. Wilderness
areas--New
York (State)--Adirondack Mountains--Anecdotes. 5. Wilderness area
users--New York (State)--Adirondack Mountains--Anecdotes. I. Title.
  SB481.6.W45A3 2005
  363.6'8'092--dc22

                                    2005010219

North Country Books, Inc.
220 Lafayette Street
Utica, New York 13502
www.northcountrybooks.com

Acknowledgments

I would like to offer a special thanks to the many friends and associates who assisted me in the preparation of this book. I owe a special debt of gratitude to my wife Patty and my mother Bernice for their patience and suggestions while proofreading the manuscript.

Barbara Remias was instrumental in providing details regarding the Interior Ranger stations, and graciously supplied many of the older photographs which appear throughout the text.

Tom Eakin provided me with the opportunity to spend time as a Wilderness Park Ranger in the West Canada Lakes region, and also arranged for my time as the Fire Observer on Pillsbury Mountain.

Shawn Dilg prepared the maps that appear in the beginning of this book. Thanks to Walter Johnson for his support.

Finally, I would like to thank John Remias (deceased) for the laughter and the companionship that made my days in the West Canada Lakes so memorable. He is sorely missed by all who knew him, and it is to his memory that this book is dedicated.

Table of Contents

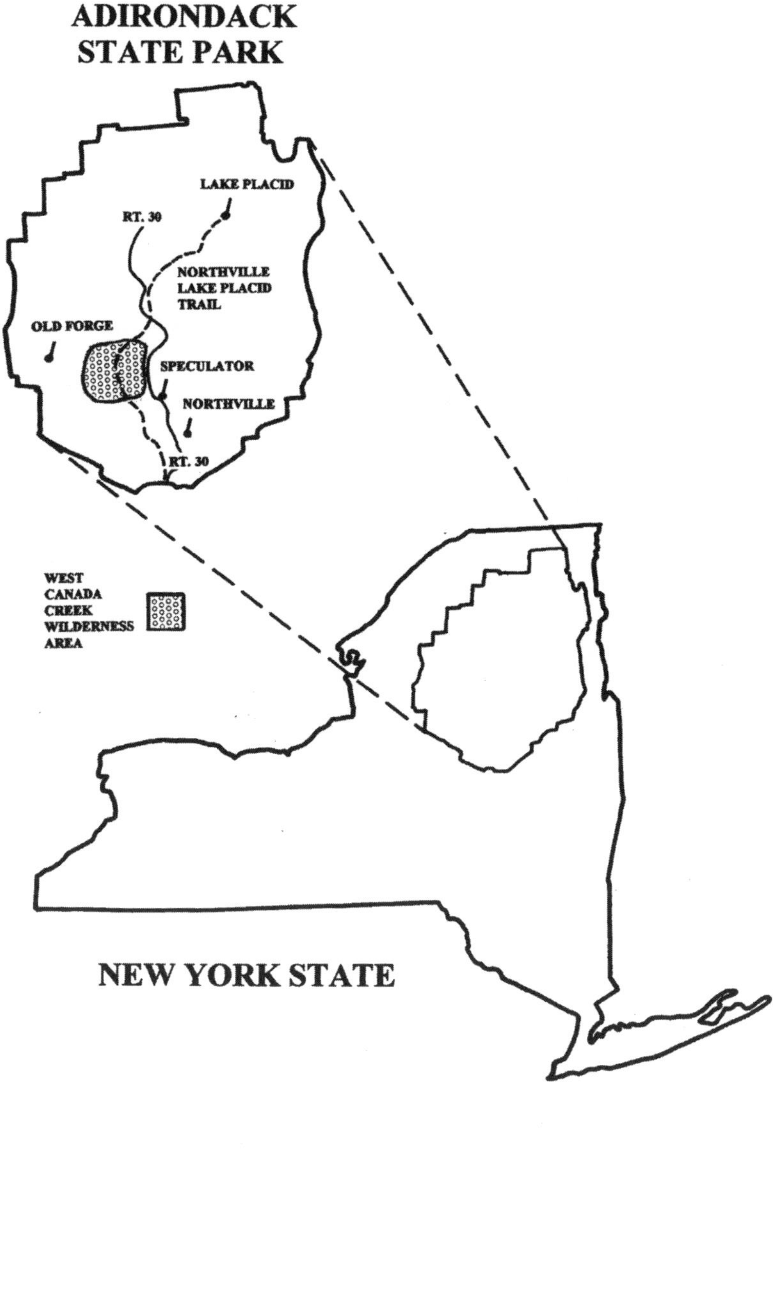

ADIRONDACK
STATE PARK

LAKE PLACID

RT. 30

NORTHVILLE
LAKE PLACID
TRAIL

OLD FORGE

SPECULATOR

NORTHVILLE

RT. 30

WEST
CANADA
CREEK
WILDERNESS
AREA

NEW YORK STATE

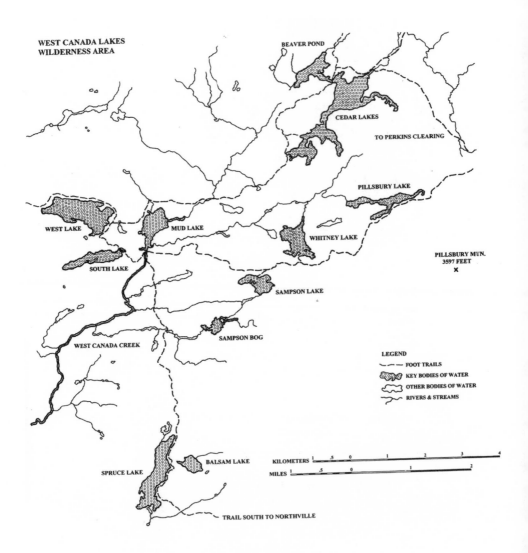

WEST CANADA LAKES
WILDERNESS AREA

BEAVER POND

CEDAR LAKES

TO PERKINS CLEARING

PILLSBURY LAKE

WEST LAKE   MUD LAKE

WHITNEY LAKE

SOUTH LAKE

PILLSBURY MTN.
3597 FEET
X

SAMPSON LAKE

WEST CANADA CREEK

SAMPSON BOG

LEGEND
- - - - FOOT TRAILS
KEY BODIES OF WATER
OTHER BODIES OF WATER
RIVERS & STREAMS

SPRUCE LAKE   BALSAM LAKE

KILOMETERS 1   .5   0   1   2   3   4
MILES 1   .5   0   1   2

TRAIL SOUTH TO NORTHVILLE

Introduction

Someone once told me that "it doesn't matter what you do for a living; just make sure that you enjoy doing it." It sounded like good advice at the time, and I've always tried to adhere to it.

True, there have been times in my life when I've gotten stuck in the day-to-day drudgery that accompanies most nine-to-five jobs. However, for the most part I've been able to avoid that type of work, as I do not do well with schedules. As a matter of fact, I detest them!

This book is written about a time in my life when I was able to throw away the daily schedule book, and, for that matter, the weekly and monthly schedules as well. My task for this period, which extended from April of 1979 through September of 1981, was to hike the trails of the Adirondack Park in northern New York State. While doing this, I was to educate the public about such varied concerns as safety, land use, and campsite regulations.

For any readers who are not familiar with the Adirondack Park, it is difficult to describe quickly. The vital statistics state that the park itself is about 6.3 million acres in size. This translates to a square which measures almost 100 miles on each side, and an area larger than seven states.

But nowhere in these numbers can one detect the incredible beauty and diversity of these lands. From the sheer outward magnificence of the High Peaks to the quiet solitude of the low-land meadows, the Adirondack Park has it all.

The almanac also lists the Park as having about 130,000 year-round inhabitants, the majority of whom are clustered in the picturesque towns which dot the countryside. But once again, these figures do not do justice to the hardy souls who have eked out a meager subsistence in this harsh, rugged territory. The residents are tough, resilient individuals who have overcome the elements (both natural and man-made), and developed into the entrepreneurs of today.

My few years of employment as a Wilderness Park Ranger brought me face to face with many of these fascinating personalities. It also introduced me to a variety of back country park users, a spectrum that extended from the old-time hunters and trappers on one extreme to the "city-slicker" hikers, hippies, and genuine nut cases on the other.

This compilation of tales, reflections, and recollections is their story. It brings back many happy memories of a simpler time in my life. And, although many of the old-timers who blessed my existence back then are now gone, the Adirondack lands and lakes that were so well described in the writings of William Chapman White remain intact.

It is my sincerest hope that your journey through these episodes will be as enjoyable for you as it was for me.

—1—

The Interview

Oh, hell. What could I possibly have been thinking to prompt me to dress up like this for a job interview as a ranger? I must have been out of my mind.

I sat quietly in the corner, looking around at the other candidates who had come to interview for the Wilderness Park Ranger position. They were all rugged looking young men and women, dressed in heavy work shirts and thick wool pants. Most of them looked as though they'd be ready to walk out the back door of the Department of Environmental Conservation (DEC) building and directly onto the trail.

But not me, I selected a different style of apparel for the interview, and was clad in a three-piece suit. And not just your average conservative business suit, no, mine was made of a tan crushed velvet, with the extremely wide lapels popular back in the mid 1970s. The wide, paisley tie that I chose to go with my outfit that morning stood out like a beacon beneath my tightly buttoned vest. I looked as though I'd be more at home in a discotheque than in the wild forests of the Adirondacks. I noticed the other candidates glancing at me suspiciously. My spirits plummeted.

Not that I had a lot of confidence coming into this selection process in the first place. As a matter of fact, I still believed that I had made it that far due to my being a "graduate student in forest biology" at the State College of Environmental Science & Forestry at Syracuse. What I failed to mention on my job application was that I was soon to become an ex-graduate student of forest biology. My grade point average had fallen below the minimum required to stay in school, and I was being asked to withdraw from the program. In other words, I needed a job.

That's when I saw the advertisement, and it couldn't have come at a better time. As a matter of fact, sitting there in the living room of my apartment, it seemed too good to be true, and I almost discarded it without applying.

In big, bold letters it said: WANTED—Young men and women who enjoy hiking and camping in one of the country's largest and most spectacular state parks. Must be able to endure fresh air and incredible scenery for extended periods of time, and be willing to receive a paycheck for doing so.

Well, the advertisement didn't read exactly like this, but it might as well have. It was the type of listing that attracts masses of applications, usually for too few openings, and I, being young and foolish, decided to join the masses of applicants, although I was certain that I had absolutely no chance of being selected.

Curiously, the events leading up to this chapter in my life could be categorized as one huge coincidence, the kind that you'd hear about on a Paul Harvey show.

In the summer of 1978, I was introduced to the Adirondack Park and the High Peak region by Pat Longabucco, a good friend and fellow graduate student at the College of Forestry. One bright June afternoon, we climbed Phelps Mountain, a small but beautiful peak with outstanding views of Mt. Colden and several nearby impressive peaks. Standing on the rock summit that day, I knew that I had to return to this place. I was hooked.

Later that same summer, I made two more trips to the High

Peaks area, climbing Mount Colden and Mount Marcy. These two popular peaks are usually on the "first to climb list" for most hikers of the High Peaks area. Mount Marcy receives the lion's share of the visitors, simply because it is the highest peak in New York, at 5,344 feet. And it was there, on a cloudless August afternoon in 1978, that I unknowingly started my interview process.

Back then, Patty and I were pretty much run-of-the-mill hikers, straggling to the top of Mount Marcy like the hundreds of other visitors that afternoon. Those were the "early days" for the two of us, many years before we were married. I'm still convinced that if she had known how many mountaintops we'd visit over the next twenty years, she would have found another suitor! However, Marcy was the first peak that she ever climbed, and as such she was still an unsuspecting accomplice.

Once on top, we met and began talking with a High Peaks Wilderness ranger by the name of John Giedraitis. We had a lengthy discussion about my research work at Syracuse, while he casually described his job in the Park. He was a pleasant individual who was obviously in love with his work. And it was easy to see why. Who wouldn't be excited about working and living in such a setting? I personally would've taken that job for free.

In any case, we thoroughly enjoyed our climb, and then returned to Syracuse and the hustle bustle of everyday life in the city. The trip up Marcy became just a memory, and the details of our conversation with the ranger on top began to fade.

It was the following year, right after the holidays, when I heard a knock on the door. This was good, as we'd just advertised for a roommate in our apartment. We were, to put it mildly, short on bucks, and needed to find someone quickly.

The fellow who walked in represented the ideal, all-American stereotype of a straight-arrow. He was well-groomed, neatly dressed, and appeared to be in excellent physical condition, as though he was a long distance runner.

As we talked about the apartment, I began to notice something familiar about the man. I couldn't put my finger on it, but I felt as though I had talked with him before.

Evidently, he felt the same way, because about ten minutes into our conversation he looked at me quizzically and asked, "By any chance, have you ever climbed in the High Peaks of the Adirondack Mountains?"

It was John! The very same ranger who had shared his experiences with us on top of Marcy had now showed up at our door in Syracuse, looking for a room. He even recalled the details of our conversation from that summer day, which is more than I could claim.

John lived with us that winter, bringing with him a virtual warehouse of interesting stories from his days as a wilderness ranger. He was a gifted storyteller, and often occupied our snowy Syracuse evenings with tales of the woods. I must admit that I was probably a good subject, being quite content with listening to as many of these episodes as John could recall.

It was sometime around February of 1979 that things began to happen. John received a notice of the start date for the 1979 ranger season, which would employ him from April through November. He was guaranteed the job, since he had held it the year before. Included in the letter was a description of the application process for any of the newly created ranger positions, which would be filled by the formal interview process the following month.

John looked over the forms, and then passed them across the small kitchen table to me. "Why don't you apply for one of these?" he asked, as though getting hired was a done deal. "They're looking for people to work a bunch of new areas outside the High Peaks. I wouldn't mind trying a few of them out myself."

I looked at him rather incredulously. "Me? How could I possibly get that kind of a job? Surely they're looking for people who are more 'woodsy' than I. Besides, every hiker and his brother are probably applying for it."

But John would not back down, and I soon handed him my

completed application form. I thought it was a useless proposition, but then again a postage stamp cost only fifteen cents back then, so why not send it in.

I was amazed at the response, which arrived at the house just a few weeks later. I had been selected as one of the finalists, and was invited to attend the selection interview at the Department of Environmental Conservation headquarters in Warrensburg, NY later that month. This was getting serious!

I remember very little about the trip up to Warrensburg on that chilly March morning. The temperature had warmed up into the low teens, and the snow was plowed into deep piles surrounding the entry to the building.

Upon entering the front doorway, I found myself face to face with the other "finalists." It didn't help to think that, of the twenty-five positions available, thirteen were being filled by returning rangers. There would be only twelve new hires from the entire group there that day. I didn't feel too confident.

I was in awe. Most of the other men and women present looked like real-life versions of Grizzly Adams. I could easily see them having vast amounts of experience on the trails, building log shelters with one hand, while they dispatched a herd of woolly mammoths with the other. What chance did I have? I was a graduate student with no beard and a positively miserable grade point average. And to top it off, I was the only one in the room dressed in a crushed velvet suit—ready to walk off the set of Saturday Night Fever.

Before long, we were gathered in a large meeting room, where we received a preview of the selection process. We were also informed that they had received over three-hundred applications, which had been narrowed down to the fifty individuals present in the room.

From here, we would wait until our name was called, then proceed into the interview room. I remember feeling a little bit nervous, but not overly tense, as I really didn't think that I had much of a chance when compared to most of these modern day Daniel Boones. I'd just go in there and give it my best.

It was one of the more unusual interviews I've ever had, before or since that time. Upon being called into the room, I was seated in a chair facing a table, on the other side of which sat five or six forest rangers. I was also conscious of about four or five other DEC administrators who were seated in back of me. Well, this would be interesting! Gang interviews! I could just picture the post interview "thumbs up/thumbs down" count.

My watch told me the entire interview lasted only about ten minutes, yet it seemed like hours. I actually thought I'd done O.K. I felt as though I'd answered everyone's questions to their satisfaction, and hopefully I'd made myself appear to be as woodsy as a native of New Jersey could be! Now, it was just a matter of waiting until they made it through all of the remaining candidates, which would take a couple of hours.

I didn't stick around, deciding to kill some time by going out for a sandwich. I wanted to do something relaxing, as I was developing an even more pronounced case of the jitters. After all, I was really beginning to believe that I had a chance at getting this thing.

And I did want it very badly, as my efforts in completing a graduate degree at Syracuse had fallen far short. Since this job related to forestry, it would be a good way of "saving face." It would also be a great way to go camping for the season while getting paid for it, which sounded like a splendid idea to me.

The interviews lasted well into the afternoon. After the final candidate was interviewed, we were once again gathered together and thanked for our interest. Meanwhile, the interview panel was comparing notes and adding up the scores, deciding who would be hired and who would not. It was time to panic.

Then, we saw the list. It was written on a simple piece of notebook paper, held in a poised hand. In a rather unusual procedure, the DEC representative began to read the names of those individuals who were not selected. I held my breath as each name was read out loud, hoping that mine would not be next. The dejected ones turned and walked from the room one by one.

The roll call seemed to go on forever, with name after name being read in a monotone voice by the ranger in charge of the ordeal. And then, as suddenly as it had started, it was over. I opened my eyes and looked around me. My name had not been called, and I was left standing there with a small knot of some other very relieved looking individuals.

We had made it!

I learned shortly that I had not been chosen to serve in the High Peaks region, which was considered by everyone to be the real prize position. Instead, I was selected by a ranger named Tom Eakin, and I would be stationed in the West Canada Lakes Wilderness area. This tract, located in the South Central region of the Park, was a vast, sprawling desolate region of lowland lakes and streams. It covered some 165,000 acres of territory, which was surrounded by additional forest lands to the north (by the Moose River Plains), and to the south (by the Silver Lakes wilderness area).

I thought that I detected a few sympathetic glances directed my way by some of the High Peaks people. The word was out that my job would be a very lonely one, with few if any people making it back to the area. There would be one other wilderness ranger back there, but we'd probably never see each other.

Then, I was introduced to Ben Woodard, who had filled my position the previous year. He was vacating it in order to move up to one of the High Peaks jobs, and clearly wanted to put my mind at ease about my new responsibilities.

Ben was the picture of what you'd expect to see in a lumberjack turned ranger. He was tall, muscular, and fit. He always seemed to wear a smile, which reflected his friendly, outgoing personality. There was no doubt as to why he was such a popular figure on the trails.

"Larry, you're going to one of the most spectacular areas in the entire Adirondack Park," he stated earnestly. "And you'll have it all to yourself, because you won't have to worry about the crowds of people that we do. Its true wild Adirondacks, the way it was a hundred years ago. In a way, I almost feel like going back there again myself."

Well, the day had turned out perfectly. I had gotten the job, and was on my way towards a seven-month tour of some very remote territory. Little did I know at the time I would remain in that region for the next three years, finding it too beautiful to leave.

Things were looking good.

2

Training Week

Park Ranger training week was a good idea. It was the state's way of getting us all together for a short, five-day period of time when we could receive "the knowledge," sort of a crash course on regulations, first aid, and public relations all in one injection.

For the Park Rangers, it was also a nice social event, especially for those returning rangers who had become friends the previous year. There were a total of twenty-five men and women who would be on the job that season, and about half of them were entering their second year as Park Rangers.

The "head instructor" for our week of indoctrination classes was the well known High Peaks forest ranger C. Peter Fish. Pete, who is retired today, was custom made for the job. He patrolled his territory on an extremely active schedule. As a matter of fact, it's almost scary. I once mentioned that I'd been up the 5,114-foot Algonquin Mountain that week. Algonquin is the second highest peak in New York State, and requires some amount of stamina and endurance to climb. After listening to me for a few minutes, Pete mentioned that he'd have to get up there himself, because he "hadn't been there since last Friday!"

Our accommodations for that week were superb. The state had arranged rooms for us in the Saranac Hotel, located about fifteen miles from our training site at Heart Lake. The Saranac is a grand hotel run by the students of Paul Smith's College's, School of Restaurant Management. The rooms were comfortable, the service was friendly and the food was more than adequate.

The classroom training sessions were held in the hikers building at Heart Lake, nearby the Adirondack Lodge. On the other side of the parking lot was a popular trailhead for hikers aspiring to climb Mount Marcy, Algonquin, or numerous other Adirondack High Peaks.

One individual who I particularly wanted to get to know was John Wood. John was the other ranger selected for the West Canada Lakes Wilderness area that summer, making him my partner. We had a lot to talk about.

John was the exact opposite of Ben, our predecessor from the previous year. John was fairly short and wiry, and looked as though he could hike all day without fatigue. He seemed fairly quiet, and occasionally lit up a wood-briar pipe which added to his persona. He possessed a thorough knowledge of the many state regulations and policies regarding land use in the Adirondack Park. I was quite impressed.

I'm not really sure that John was equally as impressed with me, and with good reason. I was new to the region, having hiked very little in the Adirondacks. Also, I was carrying around some extra weight, having enjoyed too much pizza and beer while attending classes at Syracuse. (They were my two favorite food groups.) I didn't look entirely ready to lead a class in aerobic exercise.

The classes focused on a wide variety of topics, from regulations and law enforcement, to trail maintenance and first aid. I particularly enjoyed a course called "Mountain Medicine," which was taught by an EMT member of the White Mountain Club. They also discussed accident scene management.

After completing the first aid course, we went out into the

woods to practice what we'd learned. This would include finding and treating a "victim," then transporting them back to the lodge using a Stokes litter. The Stokes is a metal-framed wire basket that holds the injured person immobilized in a horizontal position. Handholds are provided along the outside of the frame which allows the rescuers to carry it "comfortably."

Somewhere during the early part of the week, we took a group hike up Phelps Mountain. I was glad they had picked out this particular peak to ascend, since it was one of the few that I could honestly claim to have done already. I was still feeling like quite the tenderfoot.

Sitting on top of Phelps that morning, it struck me once again what a fantastic group of individuals the state had selected. They were all knowledgeable, fun-loving, and hard-working souls who just enjoyed being there.

By the following weekend we had been issued most of our standard equipment, which included uniforms, outerwear, packs, tents, and about 300 pounds of assorted "stuff." We then drove down to a designated campground known as South Meadows, where we all set up our tents for the final night of the week. Personally, I preferred the comforts of the Saranac Hotel, but I wasn't about to voice my opinion.

It was interesting to note that very few of the Park Rangers in attendance were planning on using many of the state-issued items. Almost everyone, for example, had their own packs and tents which they had grown accustomed to. Everyone, that is, except for me. I could've broken out my 1967 Boy Scout canvas pack, but I doubt that anyone would have been overly impressed. I opted for the state gear.

We wrapped up our training sessions early in the weekend, and then traded goodbyes. We wouldn't see each other until "halfway through the season meeting," which would be several months down the road.

I do remember looking forward to that meeting, for a number

of reasons. First of all, I genuinely enjoyed the company of this entire group of outdoorsmen. They were just fun to be around. Secondly, I'd feel more at ease by then, as I'd have a little bit of experience under my belt.

3

Final Preps

We drove in tandem from the High Peaks training session to our newly assigned territories. I had somehow managed to keep my 1971 Oldsmobile on the road, despite its efforts to self-destruct. The vehicle's odometer read over 115,000 miles, and it showed. The windshield leaked, the engine burned oil, and the front passenger door did not open. Perhaps the only good feature about the relic was that it was painted a deep red-brown, which made the large rust spots less noticeable.

Our destination on that sunny April afternoon was Northville, NY, where we were to meet our new boss at the DEC headquarters. The Northville office was in charge of Region 10, which extended through Fulton and Hamilton Counties. The building itself sits on the main road in town, next to a scenic lake that is popular with the local duck population.

We arrived fairly early in the day, as we had left Lake Placid immediately after breakfast. Tom Eakin was already there, taking care of some administrative duties. He was (and remains today) a very busy man, with a lot of territory to manage.

The Regional Forester was a middle-aged man by the name of

Delos Mallette. Delos was in charge of the entire Northville head-quarters operation. He was also one of the nicest individuals whom I had the pleasure of working with during my tenure as a Park Ranger. Although usually swamped by mountains of forms and files, he always had the time to talk about our work in the woods.

Shortly after lunch, Tom put us to work making indestructible versions of our topographic maps, which was quite a process. As anyone who has ever used a standard, 30' quadrant map knows, they fall apart quickly with even the most modest amount of use. Any moisture will cause the topographical features to rub off, especially if the map comes in contact with a rough surface.

Crease lines on these charts also cause a problem, as they invariably tear along the wear lines as they get old and used. I once witnessed a hiker on the Northville-Placid Trail holding a "map" that had disintegrated into a collection of rectangular pieces resembling a deck of cards. It reminded me of a trick that my father used to do on long car trips. As we proceeded slowly across the states, he'd tear off those portions of the map that were no longer needed, tossing the refuse into the back seat.

Tom showed us how to affix the topographical maps of our territory to large sheets of sturdy cloth, thus creating a perma-nent version. Then, we laid out our weekly patrol routes, includ-ing as many of the popular camping areas as possible.

Tom's main concern was providing coverage for the lengthy stretch of the Northville-Placid Trail that dissected the West Canada region. This meant having one of us at Cedar Lakes on any given evening. The Cedar Lakes' caretaker's cabin had been burned down by the state a few years earlier, but many hikers still expected it to be there.

We decided on a weekly schedule that allowed John to take Monday and Tuesday off each week, while my "weekends" were Wednesday and Thursday. Tom had devised a series of circular patrol routes, using several of the feeder trail systems. It would allow us a great deal of flexibility, while keeping us strategically located in case of an emergency.

One other thing that I noticed from the layout was that John and I would not cross paths but three or four times all summer. This could get lonely.

We collected the last of our gear and then proceeded to leave. I would be the first one to start a route, while John would enter the woods two days later.

I remember taking one long, final look at the heavy-duty maps that we had created that afternoon. In scanning the wilderness area depicted, I was struck by the huge amount of untouched land, without as much as a single road or dwelling for miles. The contour lines flowed around countless lakes, ponds, and steams. They ran in tight patterns of parallel lines signifying deep ridges, and they occasionally vanished completely amidst broad expanses of wet marshlands.

It looked huge, empty, and barren. And soon, very soon, it would be home.

—4—

Mountain Attitudes

People change when they enter woods.

I'm not exactly sure just what that statement means, but they do. I've observed it a hundred times, with countless individuals. A person may be a doctor, an accountant, or a high-volume marketing rep, but once they set up camp in the middle of nowhere, they are noticeably different.

Sometimes this process takes several days, and it's interesting to see the two to three day transformation that turns the high-pressure salesman into a friendly lean-to companion. The first day is usually a dead loss, or a "write-off," in financial lingo. The wake-up alarm goes off, and the annotated schedule of chores is printed off of the portable ink jet printer. (OK, so I've never actually witnessed a computer printer being carried into the woods. But, I've seen some written agendas that would compete with the most efficient business meeting schedules.) It's almost scary to watch.

As I said, this type of mentality quickly vanishes, and is replaced by the "go with the flow" mindset that is so much easier to be around. An exception to this might be the top level corporate executives whose type "A" habits are imprinted on their brains. But I really doubt they'd find the time to make it back into the woods anyway.

One type of behavior that is also fun to watch in the back-country is the stereotyped male ego. It was my wife who first pointed this out to me, although I suppose that I'd seen it before without really taking notice of it. It's there, and manifests itself in some very humorous ways.

Peter Fish actually discussed this matter during our initial ranger training sessions. In fact, it was an important part of our "Woods Psychology 101" course. The main lesson was this: Never "educate" the father of a family in front of the other family members. The same goes for boyfriends with girlfriends, because it just doesn't work. The matter gets even stickier if there are any little tots around, watching Dad blaze the trail ahead.

There are exceptions to the rule, of course, when immediate safety concerns take priority over potential bruised egos. For example, the time I came across a Boy Scout leader who was trying to accelerate the fire-starting process with a can of white gas. But, fortunately, cases like that were few and far between. Normally, we were able to follow Pete's guidance on dealing with the "top dog's" ego.

In retrospect, this was very valuable advice, because our job was to enforce the laws and educate the public while staying on good terms with our customers, the hikers. Dad had to remain infallible, and any suggestions that we made were offered as alternatives to his already near-perfect system. This led to some rather interesting situations.

One episode that summarizes this phenomenon nicely took place on one of my days off. I had left the West Canada Lakes area and had driven north to the High Peaks region. I planned on going up Skylight Mountain as a nice "busman's holiday," since there was no real climbing to be done in my own territory.

It was late in June, and the day was perfect. I ended up going over both Skylight and Mount Marcy, although the latter was un-planned. What an experience. It was the first time I had ever heard of anyone being on top of Mount Marcy in good weather without encountering any other hikers on the summit. A single-engine tour plane flew over, dipping one wing in response to my wave.

I left the top after an hour of solitude, departing only when a group of hikers arrived. I was ready to go, as it was becoming quite windy on top. Even in my wool jacket and insulated vest, I was beginning to shiver.

About one mile down from the summit, I met an upward-bound family trudging wearily along. The father and mother both were in their early thirties, while their exhausted son looked to be about seven. They were all dressed in T-shirts, shorts, and sneakers. I also noticed that there wasn't a single day pack among the three of them. Uh-oh.

I never wore a uniform while hiking on days off. However, some of my clothes were state-issued, and I could probably pass as a park ranger if I felt the situation warranted, and I decided this one clearly did.

"Hi. How y'all doing today?" I started off. As usual, I wanted to make friends before offering any helpful hints.

"We're going to climb the biggest mountain in the state!" cried the youngster, who quickly scrambled to the front. His feet were soaked, and his thin cotton shirt was dripping wet from the perspiration of the climb.

"Well that's good," I countered, trying to direct my response to the father. "You've sure got a nice day for it, except it's awful-ly cold up on top. I was even cold wearing my winter jacket. I hope you've got some pretty warm clothes with you."

The father looked at me confidently and replied, "Oh, not really, but we're only going up there to look around for a while, then we're coming back down." Meanwhile, I caught his wife star-ing longingly at the canteen that hung from my waist strap. Obviously, water was an overlooked commodity with this group.

"Is there anything to drink up on top?" she asked hopefully.

I'm not really sure of what I was supposed to say. The last time I checked, the DEC hadn't quite gotten around to placing soft drink machines on the summits of the various High Peaks.

"No, and there's no water between here and the top, either. Didn't you folks bring along anything to drink?" I knew the answer before asking the question.

The father's response to my rhetorical question was one of the most puzzling statements I ever heard during my tenure in the woods. Reaching behind his back while beaming a triumphant smile, he said, "No, but that's OK, because we have a map!" As he said this, he extracted a soggy document from his back pocket and held it up for all to see.

For a full five seconds, I stared at him, unable to speak. Maybe it was just me, but I couldn't make the connection between having a map and not having water. Even his son was baffled, looking at him with his head tilted to one side.

Maybe he was planning on wringing the perspiration out of the map, which wouldn't have been a bad idea. It looked positively drenched, and was probably useless for its intended purpose.

Things were going downhill in a hurry. The young father's smile was rapidly turning into a scowl. I had to try a different tact, and quickly.

"Well, have a nice day," I offered. Then I turned back down the trail and continued my descent. At that moment, I vowed to never again mess with the male ego. At least not on my day off.

—5—

Summer Distractions

It was hot. I mean really hot, one of those July days when the heat seems to bake right through the trees and get you, even when you're standing in the shade.

It very seldom got that uncomfortable back in the woods. For one thing, the trees provided a fairly nice blanket of shade over the trails and camping areas. I often had friends comment about my lack of a suntan. Also, the entire area was a bit raised in elevation, which contributed to the slightly lower temperatures.

But that particular summer day the heat was unmerciful, broiling the ground into a hard brown crust. The wind had disappeared completely, and the temperature was up in the nineties. Standing on the bridge over the outlet of Beaver Pond, I felt the sweat pouring down the inside of my shirt.

I remember feeling tempted to cast my duties aside for a while and dive into the lake, despite the fact that I never carried a swimsuit with me. I must admit though, it was tempting just to think about it.

I was in that thought process when I heard footsteps behind me. I turned and saw a couple approaching me, a man and a woman, strolling along in single-file. Both appeared to be in their twenties and in good physical condition. They strode over the faded boards of the bridge to where I was standing.

"Excuse me, but could you tell us where the Cedar Lakes Caretaker's cabin is?" asked the young man. He was tall, with light brown hair and blue eyes, and wore a friendly expression.

I couldn't resist giving him my standard response: "Well, just keep going north, and head down that trail about three years ago. You'll come right to it." And this was somewhat of an accurate answer, as the caretaker's cabin had been located a short distance up the trail before it was burned down by the state three years earlier.

After explaining my odd directions to him, we settled into a nice conversation. They were a brother-sister combination who was hiking the entire Northville-Placid Trail. They had been looking forward to seeing the cabin that had been so beautifully described in their guidebook. Sadly, it was a topic that came up often with other hikers as well.

Their names were Kevin and Karen, and they were both first-time visitors to the region. Looking at Karen, I could see the family resemblance with her brother. She had light brown hair that fell across the shoulders of a yellow cotton shirt. Her eyes were the same shade of blue as her brothers, and were framed in an attractive face. I tried not to stare.

We stood on the bridge for some time, as Kevin was telling me about their efforts to locate the lean-to on Third Cedar Lake. As he talked, I was becoming acutely aware of his sister's actions. She was disrobing.

What is she doing, I thought to myself. Maybe she's just changing her shirt. She must be overheated, with all this heat and humidity. While Kevin talked about the trail, Karen peeled off her outer garments, revealing a tube top that refused to meet her hiking shorts. Well, at least she was still covered, which was just as well for me. I've always been one of those people who blushed easily.

Kevin kept up his conversation about the area, and wanted to know more about my job as a Park Ranger. He struck me as a nice fellow who was a bit of a bookworm. I was about to respond to his query when I heard a metallic tinkling noise from off to my left side. It sounded an awful lot like a belt buckle coming undone. I glanced back at Karen.

Yup, that's exactly what it was.

This time, it was her hiking shorts. I was becoming uncomfortable. Kevin was obviously used to this, and continued as though nothing was happening.

Through my peripheral vision, I had one more peek. A tiny pair of pink panties and a white, microscopic tube top, on top of a very tall, athletically shaped body. She had nothing else on.

I wasn't just blushing, I was in full color.

I felt compelled to answer Kevin's questions, although I was distracted and stammering badly. Still, I tried. "Yes, this job can be a bit tough," I continued. "I have to carry two weeks nude, I mean food, with me at all times."

It went downhill from there. I'm certain that Kevin thought that I had a serious speech impediment, as my conversation had degenerated into a series of mumbled gibberish that sounded like something being read from the Dead Sea Scrolls. I was also aware of the extra beads of perspiration that had formed across my brow. I must have been a sight.

Off to the side, I thought I heard the remaining articles of clothing being removed, followed by a loud splash. I dared not look. I just wanted to get out of there.

But before leaving, I did want to warn them of the dangers of over-exertion on a hot day like that. After all, the high humidity and extreme heat had caused several cases of heat exhaustion in the past. Education was part of my job, and I considered myself to be quite the professional.

I took a deep breath to compose myself, and faced the water so as to address both of them simultaneously.

"Good luck on the rest of your hike," I said calmly. I had prudently focused my eyes on Kevin to start my farewell. "And please be careful of this heat. It can really sap your strength."

Not wanting to ignore Karen completely, I turned my eyes in her direction. She was treading water directly in front of me, looking up at the bridge.

Birthday suit.

I knew that I had to continue, and without stammering, "And remember to drink plenty of water and take frequent breasts, no, no I mean rests."

All was lost, and I beat a hasty retreat.

—6—

Long Island Folks

Uh oh. This one was going to be a challenge.

I was mildly surprised to see the shiny new green tent, freshly erected on the slope that bordered the northern shore of Cedar Lake. After all, it was a Tuesday afternoon in late September, and I rarely saw anyone on weekdays once Labor Day had passed. Weekends were still busy times, but somehow I doubted that my presence was really needed from Monday through Friday.

This was a first. I can truly say that this was the only tent I'd ever seen with its own "turf" staked out. And I do mean staked out. Surrounding the square-shaped tent was an even larger square, perhaps fifty feet on each side, of real estate that had been roped-off with heavy-duty twine. No barbed-wire or guard dogs were evident, but I did quickly check for their presence as I approached the installation.

The four campers were dressed in the latest combat-camping apparel, which evidently mandated a minimum of three army-style survival items, along with a machete which must have exceeded two feet in length.

As I closed in on the perimeter of the camp, I was able to

make some quick observations about the defenders. They were all in their early-to-mid twenties, and appeared to be in fairly good shape. They all spoke with a pronounced Long Island accent, which I detected while overhearing two of them arguing over who should've brought the toilet paper. Not a good start.

Perhaps I could help.

"Howdy!" I shouted, in my best Andy Griffith-style welcome. "How y'all doin'?" I often found that my best approach in cases like this was to act like a neighbor with an extra apple pie to share. Acting like the resident figure of authority just didn't cut it, at least not right off the bat.

Two of the four visitors ambled over towards the newly laid property line. They were apparently not hostile, and even offered a handshake in greeting. Meanwhile, the other two continued their task of reinforcing the campsite defenses.

"Hi ya'" came the response from the taller of the two. "You the ranger around here?" It was a question that suggested a desire for information about the area. This was not unusual, as a majority of the hikers coming through our region were first-time visitors.

We spoke for some time, and it became obvious that they were total neophytes to the outdoor arena. Uncle Tony had bought one of them a tent, which may have been an attempt to get them out of the house for the weekend. However, it clearly was a two to three man tent, and not a very large one at that, certainly not large enough to house all four of them.

Yep, this would be interesting.

I waited until we had talked for ten minutes or so before asking the question: "So tell me, what's the string around the campsite for? I don't believe I've ever seen anyone else do that before." It was as harmless an inquiry as I could come up with at the time. Besides, I really did want to know.

"Oh, we just wanted to make sure that we got a good campsite to stay in for a couple of days. We heard that the campgrounds can get a bit crowded at times, and we really didn't want to be tripping over someone else's tent strings at night," came the reply from Greg, who had introduced himself as a tool and die maker. He seemed like a fairly decent fellow, as did the others. In fact, by now they were all interested in talking about the geography of the area, which was a good sign.

Anyways, my suspicions had been confirmed. This was their plot of land, and trespassing by other campers was clearly not to be tolerated.

It took a while to get through to them that their impromptu fence was probably not necessary. In fact, with the exception of me, they were probably the only members of their species within ten miles. However, this is a tough concept for anyone from a big city to accept, and I finally took leave to return to my lean-to, which was located about a mile away from their site.

I was in the process of preparing my evening meal when they arrived, all four of them, with gear in hand.

"Our tent's too small," barked Paul, who was one of the more soldier-like members of the group. "You got room in the lean-to for a few more people?" It actually sounded more like a demand than a question, but I really didn't mind. Most of the lean-tos built in the West Canada Lakes area hold at least six people, with gear. Besides, I usually enjoyed having company around, as it allowed me to get better acquainted with more of the park's users.

It turned out that all four of them worked in the town of Jericho, NY, and had been friends since high school. This outing was something that they had wanted to do for a long time, and they were making the most of their "wilderness expedition." There was quite a bit of machismo running around, with each of them trying to "out-woodsman" the other.

Unfortunately, they were quite inexperienced in just about every facet of hiking and camping. Their dinner, which came out of one huge can, was placed in a kettle directly on the coals, and quickly turned into an amorphous black blob of crusty material that bore an amazing resemblance to anthracite. It was given a stately burial, which reduced their feast to a batch of baked potatoes and a jar of peanut butter.

During dinner, Greg stepped back into the lean-to and retrieved some of his wet clothing that he wanted to dry out. Unfortunately, it was all cotton, which is well known for its ability to retain moisture. Drying it completely would be difficult.

However, Greg was up to the challenge, and he neatly draped his soggy blue jeans, shirt, and socks over the rocks that lined the fireplace. This usually worked, as long as the fire's not too hot, or the clothes aren't placed too close to the flames. Greg, however, didn't pay too much attention to small details like this. Instead, he dumped extra wood on top of the fire, which quickly increased in intensity. As the flames rose, I could feel the heat reflecting back onto my face. It was hot.

It was perhaps a bit too hot, as I noticed steam rising from the heavy blue jeans which were a good foot from the nearest flame. He had placed his shirt and socks even closer to the blaze, and I was wondering just how long it would take before they became part of the inferno.

It wasn't long. As Greg and his companion fought over the amount of hot chocolate powder that should go into each cup, I watched the first fibers of material start to glow a pretty orange color. The flickering embers on the cloth turned into a steadier flame, which began climbing up the rapidly disappearing fabric. I felt that I really ought to say something.

"Excuse me, Sir... you're socks are on fire!" was all that I could blurt out. Even as the words emerged from my mouth, I realized how odd it must have sounded. But it did get the job done, as a rather panicked Greg jumped over the wood pile and kicked his charred athletic socks off of the rocks. In the background, his friends were in hysterics.

Burnt socks smell absolutely terrible. They were buried in a gravesite near the anthracite slab.

Once dinner was over and Greg's socks had been laid to rest, the gang congregated around the campfire for an evening of conversation and storytelling. Much of the conversation revolved around the local bear population. "How many do you see every night?" and "Has one ever tried to get into your sleeping bag?" were some of the more unusual questions that I fielded. (I must admit, I was sometimes guilty of embellishing my responses to bear questions.)

The group stayed up until quite late, telling stories about friends back home, and just generally enjoying themselves. As a matter of fact, they were enjoying themselves so much that I didn't realize just how worried they were about bears.

Then, I saw it.

It had to be the biggest gun in the world. Or perhaps, the second biggest, as I am fairly certain that the 16" guns carried on World War II battleships were a tad bit larger; not by much. I was quickly informed by Paul that it was a Winchester .458 caliber piece of "protection" that could stop an Amtrak locomotive at 1,000 yards. I believed it. Each shell looked heavy enough to require two men to lift it into the gun.

So with the gun laid carefully across the back of the lean-to, they began their final nighttime preparations, which included stoking the fire one last time. Everyone then climbed into their sleeping bags, watched the flames slowly die down, and drifted off into a quiet, peaceful sleep. The night was dark and still, without even a rustle of wind through the trees. The silence was absolute.

KABOOOOM!

I awoke in mid-air, perhaps two or three feet above the floor of the lean-to. At a later time, given time to reflect on this feat, I pondered about just how this was possible, since I had been lying flat on the wooden floor when the canon went off in my ear. In any case, there I was, awake in flight and about to start my descent. My eardrums were numb, my eyes were popping, and my heartbeat was somewhere up in the 250-300 bpm range. It was 2:00 A.M.

"Yee-haa! I got rid of that bear in a hurry!" Paul screamed from the front of the lean-to. "He tried getting to us from the water, but I heard him make a loud splash out there. I think I got him." His companions scrambled forward to see if there were any remains to view. Meanwhile, I quickly pulled on my trousers, still waiting for my heart to slow down to an acceptable rate. In the back of my mind, I kept thinking one thing: We only had one beaver living down at this end of the lake. Now I feared he was gone.

"I don't see any bear out there. Are you sure?" asked Jerry, who looked as though he was as badly shaken by the blast as I was. He was fair-skinned to begin with, and the shock of being awakened by the roar of the weapon only added to the effect. In the narrow beam of the flashlight, he looked as pale as a ghost.

"Of course I'm sure! Don't you think I know a bear when I hear one?" Paul replied indignantly. He then scanned the lake, which had become partially illuminated by a beautiful full moon. "There he is again!" he hollered, pointing to the nose that had surfaced approximately 150 feet to the west. "He's heading right for that beaver lodge over there!"

I remember thinking to myself that I was definitely being underpaid for the job.

—7—

Meeting up with John

It seems strange that in an area with so few people and so much natural beauty, that my fondest memories are of the people with whom I worked. One of my most valued friendships was to be found in the person of John Remias, the resident caretaker at West Canada Lakes caretakers' cabin.

I had heard a lot about John before ever setting foot in my territory, as he had a reputation as an outstanding woodsman, hunter, and trapper. My predecessors told me of the stories he'd passed on to them about the local woods and how it had changed over the decades. He remembered the locations of the many hunting and logging camps that used to dot the landscape around the lakes in our area. Most of them had been gone for years and no visible traces remained. It seemed as though he was a walking encyclopedia.

I had been working in the West Canada Lakes for almost three weeks before I finally crossed paths with John. I was heading west along the Placid Trail, and had just crossed over the Mud Creek Bridge when I saw him on the trail ahead. John was standing on a makeshift ladder, working on the phone line that used to snake its way along the 15-mile route back into his cabin.

John looked exactly as I had pictured him: a thin, wiry frame, very short gray hair, and a slightly rounded face. The dark suntan and the three-day stubble on his chin were as I had imagined as well. He looked as though he was a natural part of the scenery that somehow "came with the territory" back there. I was eager to talk with him.

"Hello...John?" I asked, as I approached his perch on the ladder.

"Yup, that's me," he replied, looking down at me as though doing a rather rapid evaluation of what he saw.

"I'm Larry, your other trail walker," I said smiling, while extending a handshake. I used the term "trail walker" because I had the funny feeling that John didn't go for fancy titles like "Wilderness Park Ranger," or anything like that. My partner, John Wood, had met John the previous week and had filled me in on his personality.

"Yeah, I was kind of expecting you to pass by here sometime today or tomorrow. John told me that I'd be able to recognize you by the size of your pack. He was right!"

John was already poking fun at my equipment, as he wasn't a proponent of toting along any more weight than was absolutely necessary. I carried what was then the largest frame pack made in the country. It was huge.

We talked for a few brief moments, while the blackflies seemed to congregate in a massive cloud above my head. As they began descending over my eyes, ears, and mouth, I started to swat them away so as not to swallow them while breathing. John seemed to be amused by my futile attempts to disperse the flock that was making a meal out of me.

"Tell you what, there, Larry," he said while climbing down from his work. "How about we head back to the cabin and have something cold to drink? You head over there now, and I'll be along in about ten minutes or so. We can replace some of the blood that you've donated to the flies."

I didn't need to be asked twice.

John's cabin, which was actually called an "interior caretaker's cabin," was a superbly built log structure with a rock chimney and a full-length front porch. It was beautifully situated on the eastern shore of West Canada Lakes, which was usually called West Lake by most of the hikers back our way. The cabin had a large front room with a fireplace, a good-sized kitchen, a large bedroom, and a storage room on the side.

John obviously believed in maintaining the grounds, as the grass had recently been cut. A couple of smaller huts around the building that were used for storing trail equipment and signs, as well as the inevitable outhouses (plural) for John and his "guests." The lawn tapered down to meet the rocky shoreline of the lake, where a very small dock allowed John just enough access to the water to launch his rowboat.

I sat in the front yard for a short spell while waiting for John to come down the trail. In the middle of the lawn was an ancient fireplace that had been built by the legendary Adirondack French Louie shortly after the turn of the century. Louie had planned to add a large new room onto his camp for his visitors and "sports," built around the massive rocks of the fireplace. However, the rest of the construction was never completed, and the fireplace still stands as a monument to that regionally famous guide and woodsman. I always felt just a little bit of his presence whenever I stopped at that spot.

True to his word, John arrived within a short period of time. He unlocked the front door of the cabin and ushered me into the living room, which was very nicely furnished for such a remote location.

"Y'know, Larry, twenty or thirty years ago, I never would've bothered to lock this place at all." He looked at me with the haunted eyes of someone who been repeatedly harassed by inconsiderate passersby. "People used to leave the house alone, unless they were in trouble of some sort. But you just can't do that these days. The people back here have changed; they just come in, whether the door is locked or not, and take whatever they want. Sometimes, they'll damn near bust the door down, if that's what it takes."

"But surely you must have your privacy back here?" I countered. "I mean, if you just head inside and shut your door, people won't bother you, will they?"

John had a fairly lengthy laugh over that one. "You kidding me," he chuckled. "I've had people knockin' on my door at 6:00 AM, asking if I've got an outhouse here! Of course I've got a damned outhouse! What do they think that thing next to the tool shed is, my Jacuzzi?"

I learned quite quickly that John was a bit leery of the "madding crowds" of hikers that passed through during the middle of the summer. And while the number of these users remained quite low in a relative sense, I got the feeling that John would have much preferred to be completely alone, save for the resident fauna and occasional personal visitor he received. He was very friendly, but he was also a bit of a loner.

John's family lived in nearby Lake Pleasant, and his wife Barbara was often back in to visit him. Even when she was unable to be back at the cabin, they were able to talk frequently because of the phone line, which required continuous attention. I sometimes wondered what percent of John's entire workweek was spent just keeping that relic alive. I imagine that it was quite high.

The cabin had the luxury of a propane refrigerator, from which John produced a large pitcher of iced tea. I accepted a glass, and sat down at the table in the living room. As I listened, John began telling me of some of his experiences in the West Canada Lakes region.

It turned out that prior to accepting the post on West Lake, he had lived in the old caretaker's cabin on Cedar Lakes. It was, from all accounts, a beautiful structure that was considerably larger than his new dwelling. It sat along the northern shoreline of the lake, about a quarter mile up from the dam. However, the State of New York had ordered it burnt down about three years earlier, to comply with the policy of not allowing any four-walled structures to be situated inside of designated "wilderness" areas.

John was quick to point out the obvious inconsistencies that existed within the regulations enforced on designated wilderness lands. "What about all the lean-tos; are they really different from a small cabin?" he asked. "And if you really want to get rid of all four-walled structures, I'd better leave now, 'cause I've got a helluva lot of outhouses that I'd better take down between here and Piseco!"

John had a point. And, throughout the years that I would spend back there, I'd have to say most of the public agreed with him. Almost everyone was opposed to removing the cabins.

John also had his own views about the land that we called wilderness. "You kidding me?" he'd ask with a twinkle in his eye, "How can you call this 'wilderness' when you've got a highway (which was John's name for the Placid Trail) going through here, and a blue plastic marker nailed onto every tree in sight? If you want real wilderness, let's take down the damned markers, and then leave the trails alone, without doing all this fussing around to make sure that the hikers don't have to get their feet wet while walking through the wilderness!"

I was getting an education in a hurry. It was obvious that John was a hard working, conscientious employee who had been a bit henpecked by the many years of state rules and regulations. Finally, back in the West Canadas, he could do things more or less his way.

Most of the time.

"Y'know, Larry, sometimes it makes you mad," he grimaced. "You try and take care of things as best you can back here, and then someone turns around and stabs you in the back. I had a group come through here a few weeks ago, complaining that the lawnmower was 'ruining their wilderness experience.' They even reported me to the office in Northville, so I got a call telling me not to use the lawnmower anymore. What do they expect me to do; go out with damned pruning shears and cut the grass by hand? I've got half a mind not to cut it at all, and then see how they like pushing their way through three-foot-tall wet grass every morning."

"Well, what are you going to do?" I asked. "You're going to have to do something else to keep the growth down in the clearing back there."

John laughed as he crushed out a cigarette. "Oh, no, don't worry about that; I'll use the lawnmower all right. It's always been like that back here. I just tell them 'yes, yes, yes' whenever they make up any of their new rules that don't make any sense. Then, as soon as they're gone, I just go about my business, and everyone's happy."

That made perfect sense to me, although I'm not certain as to how the "people in the office" would've felt about it. Over the years, I discovered that John always found ways to get the job done with the least possible expenditure of energy. He once encapsulated this strategy to me by citing that "you'll never see a dog stand up if it can sit down, and you'll never see him sit down if he can lie down."

He was also quite amused by my "rig," as he referred to my pack. As I mentioned earlier, I carried a huge frame pack, and usually had enough in it to tide me over for an extra week in the woods, if needed. John clearly disagreed with my strategy.

Nodding at my canteens, he asked pointedly, "What do you see in front of this cabin?"

"Well, it's West Lake..."

"And what's just south of the cabin?" John interrupted.

"Uh, South Lake," I responded sheepishly, as I realized where John was taking this little session.

"Right!" he chortled. "And we've got Mud Lake to the east, and Brooktrout Lake to the west. My suggestion to you is that you fill up those canteens with air, so that in case you fall into the water, they'll keep you and your rig afloat!"

We ended up talking for hours, and I noticed with some concern that the clock on the wall read 5:30 P.M., which meant that I only had another two to three hours of daylight left. I had spent much more time talking with John than I had intended, although I had enjoyed every moment of it, but I still had an additional four miles of hiking to do and some paperwork to fill out before fixing my evening meal. It was time to go.

As I pulled my pack onto my back and strolled away from the clearing, I glanced back over my shoulder at the old building. I had no way of knowing at that time that it would be the setting for some of the most enjoyable times I'd ever spend, and the home of one of the best friends that I would ever make.

—8—

Crossing the Jessup

During my first month on the job, Tom varied my patrol routes to maximize my exposure to the numerous trails that criss-crossed our region. It was a schedule that included four different starting points, or "trailheads," and called for an average hiking patrol of about twelve miles a day. I found this to be a comfortable amount of mileage to cover, although I also noticed it wasn't long before my clothes were fitting significantly looser from all the exercise.

By the fourth week of the season, I had covered all of the trails with the exception of the stretch of Northville-Lake Placid Trail that started in the town of Piseco and headed north, into Spruce Lake. It was a well-used path that wound its way through about twelve miles of mixed conifers and deciduous trees, often meandering up and down the many hills that dominated the landscape. Unfortunately, it was also the most eroded trail in the West Canada Lakes territory, with several portions of "four-lane highway" widths transversing the muddier sections.

I was always fascinated (and bothered) by the process that lead to these wide and eroded mud flats. The trails themselves were originally only a few feet wide, and as expected could get quite muddy during wet weather. So, in order to avoid getting dirt on their hiking boots, many hikers would actually leave the trail, traipsing over the vegetation next to the original path. This in turn converted the new detour route into mud, which pushed the hikers even further out of the intended track.

It wasn't long before many of these sections of trail were 20-25 feet wide, with vast expanses of deep mud and standing water. At times, the only solution was to spend hours of back-breaking work fitting large rocks into a virtual sidewalk arrangement that would keep the hikers on the path. And while I seldom had the time or the resources to do such construction myself, I always marveled at the handywork and imagination that went into some of the walkways and staircases built to prevent erosion in the High Peaks region.

In any case, I knew ahead of time this was going to be one wet hike. I had spent my two "off days" in Glens Falls, watching the rain come down in an unabated downpour. It never really let up, and the farmers were saying even they had received their fill of the stuff. Patty and I had given up our traditional outdoor strolls, deciding instead on a trip to the local indoor mall. Along the way to the shopping center, I noticed the roadside fields had ceased to absorb the precipitation, and that small riverettes were forming spontaneously, carrying the excess water off towards larger drainage ravines.

The following morning showed no break in the weather, and I made the ninety-minute drive to Piseco with the windshield-wipers slapping out a monotonous beat. I felt just a small bit of grumbling inside as I saddled up my pack and slid into my rain gear. On most occasions, I'd just ignore the rain, preferring the cooling moisture of a light drizzle to the stifling heat that would build up inside my full length poncho. However, this was different; it was coming down hard enough to soak through several layers of clothing in a relatively short period of time. I opted for the rainsuit.

The hike in started slowly, as I made my way along the water-soaked path. There would be no escaping the wet boots today, and I made no attempt whatsoever to tiptoe around the deeper puddles. After all, when your boots are completely saturated and you can feel the water moving between your toes, why bother stepping lightly? Live it up; jump in the puddles!

According to my maps, I'd be crossing two good-sized streams during the day. The first of these would be Fall Stream, which appeared to be about half-way through my hike. The second crossing would be the Jessup River, which had a reputation amongst the local fisherman for its productive waters. The Jessup appeared to be the larger of the two streams, and I wondered just how high the water levels would be as I attempted to ford the rapids.

One advantage to hiking through this type of rain was that I was able to observe several whitetail deer at close range. I've heard many hunters say it is easier to approach deer in rainy weather, as the background noise covers up the noise of your footsteps. Never having hunted back there, I couldn't vouch for the validity of that statement. However, I did come across several small herds during my first few hours on the trail, and even had one buck stop ahead of me on the trail, watching me intently from a distance of only about fifty feet. He must have found me to be rather uninteresting, for he soon turned away to join his companions as they sauntered back into the brush.

Within a few hours, I came upon Fall Stream, which was moving quite briskly and had overflowed its banks. The creek-side campsite was partially submerged, and a makeshift fireplace that had been built to hold small campfires was instead holding back the tide of swollen waters from the stream.

Deciding not to waste any time, I immediately crossed over to the other side of Fall Stream, where the trail resumed its route towards Spruce Lake. Under normal conditions, it was possible to walk over the tops of the rocks without getting wet feet, but not today. I continued my trek northward, and the rain intensified to monsoon proportions.

Within an hour after crossing Fall Stream, I started looking for the Jessup River. After all, I had been on the trail for nearly three hours already, I should be coming up on the landmark soon. Once I crossed the Jessup, I knew that I was entering the home stretch for Spruce Lake and a nice, dry lean-to. Now, where was that confounded river?

I heard it long before it came into view. It wasn't a gentle gurgling, or even a whooshing whitewater sound that first made it to my ears. No, this was something entirely different. It was more like a distant roar that could only come from a lot of water going over a lot of rocks in a hurry. I had never been to Niagara Falls, but I imagined that the sound would have been about the same.

It seemed as though I spent a long time approaching the river, with each bend in the trail accompanied by an additional increase in volume. I had never been there before, and could only imagine the size of the picturesque waterfall that I'd find when I finally got to the edge of the torrent. It must have been quite a drop, as the pounding waters sounded as though they had fallen for some distance before crashing on the rocks below. And with each step, it got louder.

Finally rounding one last bend, the trail split with one fork going to the right, and the other going straight ahead to the river. I took the short route, walking right up to the waters edge.

Uh oh. Bad news. There was no falls. The deafening roar that I'd been hearing for the past several hundred yards had been the river itself; massive, raging, and apparently uncrossable. The actual width of the water wasn't the problem. As a matter of fact, the entire river, even at its current flood stage, was probably less than thirty feet across. However, those thirty feet contained the highest, swiftest, and rockiest flow of whitewater that I had ever seen. I had no idea of how deep it was, and whether crossing it was physically possible.

Now, I have occasionally done some dumb things that should've gotten me into trouble, and this was one of them. As a matter of fact, even thinking of crossing the Jessup on foot, unassisted, was definitely the second dumbest thing that I did that very day. But enough about that, I was still fairly new on the job, and I was not about to turn around and hike back to Piseco because of a little water.

The next hour was a real battle. I'd probe a few feet into the river, trying to feel the placement of rocks and boulders, while using my walking stick as a third leg to counteract the current. At times, the water was really deep, and would have come up over my waist had I taken a faulty step.

In the back of my mind, I realized that if I fell, I would have been swept away downstream, losing my backpack and possibly sustaining major injury. I unbuckled my waiststrap to allow a quick exit from my pack, just in case I did fall, as I wanted to avoid being dragged underwater by its weight. Things were not looking good.

Several times I made it almost half-way across the cataclysm, only to be turned back by not finding a step that I was confident enough to rely on. I couldn't guess, as there was just no room for error. The rushing water tore at my ankles and legs until they felt numb, making it all the more difficult to navigate the expanse. If I could just get a little closer, I felt certain that some of the boulders would provide me sheltered footholds to reach the other side.

Finally, after an intolerable amount of time, and at least a half-dozen attempts, I made it across, using an ill-advised leap that cost me an inch or two of skin from my right kneecap. I had jumped towards a very large rock that looked solid, but was balanced precariously on another boulder. My final few steps to safety were a panicked combination of acrobatic leaps, hops, and pirouettes, mixed in with some backstroke and an occasional choice four-letter word. It was not pretty.

I stood on the other side, rubbing my wounds, and shaking a

bit from the cold water and the tension. My canteen had fallen off of my beltstrap, and was probably somewhere in Delaware by now. On top of this, I had water draining out of every inch of my clothing, including my underwear. I have no doubt that, had I taken off my boots, I might have found a small trout or two swimming around in there.

I needed a rest. I dropped my pack to the ground and turned around to face the flood that I had just crossed. It was only then that I realized that my hand was cramping from holding my walking stick so tightly.

But no matter, I had faced the raging river, and I had won. I had tackled adversity, and, though it was tough, I had come out on top. It felt good. I wanted to remember this place, to maintain a visual image of my physical conquest. I turned around in a full circle, taking a 360° mental picture of the place. And that's when I realized that crossing the river was only the second dumbest thing that I had done all day.

For just upstream, around one short bend, I could see the end of the other trail; the one that had forked to the right when I went straight. The one that didn't go directly to the edge of the river. The one that was just a little bit longer. The one that led to the newest, strongest, most beautiful bridge that I had ever seen.

It Must Be a Sign

I'm a terrible navigator. I always have been, and I probably always will be.

When finding my way around city highways and boulevards, my standard navigational technique is "stop and ask somebody." However, this method assumes that you happen to come across a knowledgeable individual who won't send you into some uncharted corner of the county. It can be a bit hit or miss, but the directions are free and I've ended up in some truly amazing places.

Navigation in the woods is quite a bit different than in the city. In some areas, such as the West Canada Lakes, there are no people to ask for directions, making some other form of navigating necessary. This may include using signs of nature, geographical landmarks, map and compass, or my favorite, the trail signs.

I've come to the conclusion that several of the methods listed above have some serious flaws. Navigating strictly by nature, for example, doesn't usually work. I know because I've tried it. I've looked for the mossy side of the tree, hoping to locate true north. What I discovered is that we had a genetically mutated moss in our area that was directionally challenged.

I also tried finding my way using the migratory habits of wild-fowl. After all, they were supposed to have an innate sense of direction, always finding south in the winter and north in the summer. And I actually thought it was going to work.

I had my chance one spring day. As I stood on the shore of Spruce Lake, my head tilted up towards the sky, I heard the flock of Canadian geese approaching. They were honking loudly, their wings beating the air to stay aloft in their characteristic V-forma-tion. It was April, so they must be heading north, right?

I aligned my body with their flight path, as I was heading north as well. Perfect! Off I went, happily whistling a tune with-out a care in the world.

Then I noticed something rather odd. The honking had increased in volume, and the flock was veering off slightly toward one side. What was causing the problem with my wildlife com-pass? I strained my neck upward, looking into the skies ahead of me. That's when I saw it.

The reason the flock was altering directions was to avoid run-ning into yet another flock of geese. But this one was larger and noisier than the first. They also had a different destination in mind, for they were flying in the opposite direction! The two flocks passed each other at a close interval, with each group probably laughing at the other for flying in the wrong direction.

So much for that idea.

Traveling by geographic landmarks, such as mountains, lakes, and streams is also challenging. Smaller hills and rises can restrict long-range visibility, making "line of sight" travel difficult.

Densely spaced trees and vegetation add to the problem, especially for the hiker carrying a large-framed pack. The thick undergrowth and tightly meshed limbs of the northern conifers provide a real obstacle course for anyone venturing into their grasp. John Remias once described an area around Cobble Hill as being "so thick that a snake couldn't get through." I never tried.

Map and compass? Well, maybe. I always carried a full set of maps and at least one compass, although I don't remember using them very often. But they did look impressive, and I always had the magnetic variation of the area in the back of my mind in case I ever had to resort to it.

Then there was "Plan B," the trail signs, nailed straight and true onto the sides of trusty ol' beech trees. How convenient! That's why 99.8% of all hikers use this as their sole means of finding their way about the woods. I was no exception.

Trail signs are interesting pieces of work, and can often be a bit confusing. They point in all kinds of directions and spout off authoritative sounding distances, such as "7.45 miles." How could they possibly be that accurate? It's mind boggling! But I "saw it on a sign," so it must be true.

I feel sorry for the poor souls who have to do the measuring. From what I've been told, they've been assigned the unenviable task of trudging through the woods with a wheeled measuring device in tow.

How precise can that device be, anyway, especially with the measuring wheel bouncing along over the rocks and boulders that decorate many of our trails? And how about the stretches of trail that go directly through submerged beaver swamps? We had several of these on some of the lesser used feeder trails. Perhaps we could have worked up an arrangement whereby the individual doing the measuring wore a pair of water skis hooked up to an odometer! It was an imperfect system.

I always thought it amusing when the distances on the signs didn't add up correctly. For example, the sign at the trailhead read as follows:

Elk Pond Lean-to	4.5 miles
Elk Mountain	7.0 miles

Fine. When hiking to Elk Mountain, you'd pass the lean-to in four and a half miles, which meant that you had another two and a half miles to go to reach Elk Mountain. But, once you got to the lean-to, you'd be greeted by another sign announcing, "Elk Mountain 3.0 miles." Where did the extra half-mile come from? It's a mystery to me!

It's even more humorous to see two signs at different landmarks pointing toward each other, each claiming a different distance to the other sign. How do they do that? (Perhaps one way was downhill!)

My particular territory was a fairly simple one to keep "marked." We had relatively few hikers, so vandalism and theft of trail signs was almost non-existent. Perhaps the greatest thieves of the trail markers were the trees themselves, which tended to "swallow" the small disks after a number of years. The outer layers of the tree would grow around the markers, bending them in half until they'd disappear completely under the bark some years later.

My cohorts in some of the higher-use areas, though, did have their hands full. From what I heard, it was in fashion to "pinch" an occasional trail sign, which would then find its way to some college dormitory wall. To avoid this problem in areas such as the High Peaks, the Park Rangers had to fix the signs well up off the ground out of reach. I've seen many signs in that region that would present a serious challenge to all but the most talented Olympic high jumpers.

Even that system's not perfect. For even without sticky-fingered hikers present, things happen and signs fall down on their own accord. When that happens, you're left to your own devices, allowed to select any form of navigation that pleases your fancy.

I remember a favorite incident which took place on a midsummer day off from work. I had come up the Opalescent River from Flowed Land in route to Four Corners. From this junction, it was possible to go south to Skylight Mountain, north to the summit of Mount Marcy, or straight ahead where the trail plunged into Panther Gorge. I was just climbing for the fun of it, and had no real destination in mind.

I had never been to that particular intersection before, but I was carrying the standard ADK map of the region, so I knew pretty much where I was. Still, I looked forward to arriving at Four Corners so I could check my guidebook with the distances posted on the trail sign. It was early in the day, but the sun was already beating down quite hard. I was hot and dripping with sweat by the time I reached the trail junction. My eyes were focused downward as I reached around to remove a canteen from my waist strap.

As I greedily gulped some water, my eyes caught a glimpse of the trail sign-post. It was sturdily constructed, sunk into the ground as to make it immovable. On it was the actual trail sign, which consisted of two boards affixed at right angles to each other. The signs named the four trails which headed off at right angles from that point. Each sign had distances and directional arrows clearly displayed.

But what really caught my eye was the piece of twine. Evidently, the sign had fallen off the post, and a concerned hiker had re-attached it using a handy length of string. It didn't work very well.

I stood there for some time that morning watching the sign revolve. It was fascinating, as I'd never seen a trail sign behave that way before. The wind was blowing steadily, and the arrows were spinning around the pole, creating an arrangement that resembled a roulette wheel.

Great! Which way to go?

Actually, it wasn't a problem, as this was one place where the natural landmarks were unmistakable. But still, I couldn't resist.

I took one final look at the whirling sign in front of me, then, I closed my eyes. I raised an arm to serve as a pointer, and then turned around three or four times in the same direction as the rotation of the sign. Then I opened my eyes.

I was looking at the top of Mount Marcy. That didn't seem like a bad idea, so off I went.

—10—

"1051, This is 1052"

I once had a hiker tell me that "I wouldn't touch your job with a ten-foot pole." That puzzled me just a bit, since she obviously enjoyed being in the woods. So what's wrong with getting paid for it?

"Oh, it's not that," she replied, sitting on the Cedar Lakes Dam with her two hiking partners. "It's just that I wouldn't want to be out here by myself, especially without a gun or a radio."

Ah ha, so it's that again!

I've always found it a bit difficult to understand, but many folks just didn't want to be "out there" by themselves. Somehow, Ma Bell never got around to installing pay telephones in the back country. The old caretakers' cabin used to have single-wire phone lines, but they were burned out by the state years ago. It's still possible to see some of the old phone line poles from time to time along the trails.

Hiking solo never bothered me, I loved the solitude of the area, although I never minded a bit of good company. And anyways, we did carry radios. We just wished that we didn't.

At that time, the DEC owned the largest, bulkiest, heaviest

radios available on the market. They were the radios from hell, and I, for one, did not enjoy them. They were about the size of an old fashioned lunchbox, and were powered by eleven (count 'em, eleven!) D-cell batteries. And then, just in case that wasn't enough to carry, we were given additional scanners that were supposed to pick up the "repeater" relay station on Blue Mountain. Yeah, right!

John and I were lucky that our Northville offices had one of the newer, lighter versions that took up much less room in the pack. But that one was issued to John, which was the only fair thing to do. If I'm not mistaken, my radio weighed more than John did, which would've been quite uncomfortable for him to carry.

We were assigned our radio call signs, which labeled me as "1052." What a pity. I though we could have been much more creative than that (i.e. "Papa Bear" and "Trail Warrior"), but we had to stick with the assignment. The numbers actually meant something, with the first two digits (10) signifying District Ten (Northville), and the second two digits corresponding to the number of the radio itself. Personally, I liked "Papa Bear" better.

So there we were, tramping around in the middle of a vast, hilly expanse of territory, carrying our not so state-of-the-art communications gear. I wanted to see how it worked, or didn't.

Unfortunately, it was usually the latter. This was not really anyone's fault. It was just a case of too big a distance, too many hills, and not enough transmitting power. Ben had warned me of this the year before, although he did have some good advice:

"Stand out on the point in front of the old lean-to near the dam on Cedar Lakes," he recommended. "Then, face south and hold the radio antennae over your head with your left hand."

"What?" I choked, startled by the seemingly absurd suggestion. "You've got to be kidding? What happens if anyone sees me? They'll think I'm playing 'Simon Says' with the frogs." I heard some of Ben's friends chuckling in the background. But this time, Ben wasn't smiling. He was making an honest remark about what

49

worked. Oh hell, this wouldn't be easy.

Theoretically, we had a whole communications net in place, with me, John, and the caretakers' cabin on West Lake, and the fire tower on Pillsbury Mountain. The tower was within ten miles of most of our patrol campsites, and had a fairly powerful radio. However, it was lacking just one thing, an observer.

The fire tower observer is that lonely soul who sits in the tower for months on end looking for fires. (This job ranks right up there with the Maytag repairman.) For some reason, they hadn't found a replacement for the last observer, who quit the previous year. So we could talk to Pillsbury Tower all we wanted, but nobody was there to listen!

We could occasionally reach the fire tower on Wakely Mountain, which was located about eight miles north of our territory. The Wakely tower was then able to relay our messages along, which was a comforting thought. At least it was a "way out" in case we came upon an injured hiker, which very seldom happened.

Some of the more interesting transmissions occurred between me and John. Or, perhaps I should say attempted transmissions, because this was one hook-up that almost never worked. I couldn't begin to count the number of times I muttered the words, "1051, this is 1052" into my microphone for the first several weeks on the job, I actually expected a response. I'd sit there, looking at the radio with hopeful glances, as though I could convince it to speak.

But alas, I gave up after a month of such attempts. By that time, I had tried everything. My radio and I were no longer on speaking terms. I had boosted the volume, adjusted the squelch, and tried all of the channels. I had even gone out and used my own money to purchase eleven fancy new alkali batteries, which was quite a necessary sacrifice on my $4.25 an hour salary—but to no avail.

At one point, John and I were no more than a mile apart, and on the same lake! I knew that if it didn't work then, it was a lost cause. After all, how could a radio signal not carry for one measly mile, and over water, no less? I could probably have yelled across that distance and been heard. It was a case of "now or never."

Unfortunately, it was never.

So off we went, carrying our heavy but silent boxes tenderly around the West Canada Lakes Wilderness, but it wasn't entirely for naught. After all, we did have the occasional conversation with Wakely Tower. And, if nothing else, the radios looked impressive sitting on the front table of the lean-to with the lights of the scanner flashing away. It added to the "officialness" of our presence.

Then, from out of the blue, came the glorious day that I'd waited for. I was setting up camp at the Beaver Pond lean-to, which is also located on Cedar Lakes, when I thought I heard something.

No, it must have been my imagination. I was in the process of breaking up a large beech branch into firewood for the coming evening. It must have been a smaller branch snapping, sending bark or debris nosily into the lean-to. Then I heard it again.

The radio! It was squawking to life. It was a voice! John's voice! Hooray! I practically pounced on top of the radio, grabbing it securely around its base.

"1052, this is 1051, over," crackled the call signs from my speaker piece. John was calling from somewhere, and by golly, I was receiving it!

"1051, this is 1052," I answered excitedly. "I read you loud and clear, John."

"This is 1051, I read you loud and clear, too," came the immediate response. "I've made a minor adjustment, and it seems to be making a big difference."

This made me stop and think for a few quick seconds. Minor adjustment? What kind of minor adjustment? After all, I thought I'd tried tweaking every possible control on the darned radio, and nothing seemed to make a difference. I had to find out what he had done that so drastically improved our communications.

"1051, this is 1052," I called. "What type of adjustment did you make?"

Once again, the response was immediate and crystal clear, "I tried changing the location of my radio. Turn around."

Slowly, I turned. There stood John, not more than thirty feet away, smiling with radio in hand. At least we had finally discovered our transmitting range.

—11—

Leighton's Hermitage

No account of my years in the West Canadas, nor any discussion of the region, would be complete without mentioning Leighton. Leighton Slack was the "Hermit of Perkins Clearing," and he was truly one of the bright points of my weekly schedule.

Ben had told me about the "old feller who lives by the side of the road" back in Perkins Clearing. According to Ben, he was a friendly and truly unique individual who I should get to know as soon as possible. "He'll even watch your car for you while you're back on the trail," Ben promised.

I must admit that my initial thoughts of meeting this regionally famous individual were not good. After all, I had been raised in the sprawling suburbs of New Jersey, surrounded by countless other surburbians. My mental image of the generic hermit (if there is such a person) was the stereotypical angry old man, with beard extending down below the belt and a six-shooter in one hand, ready for use. I didn't know what to expect.

I drove my rusting jalopy along the logging road that lead six miles back into the woods, finally entering Perkins Clearing in front of the sign-board for the Miami River lean-to. Continuing past the clearing, I bounced down the dirt and rocks of the seasonal route until I saw a shed along the lefthand side of the road. It matched the description that Ben had given me, so I stopped and got out of the car.

Leighton's house was a fairly small building, measuring perhaps thirty feet by twenty feet, with a small garage built in the back. It was very modest, but then again, it was apparently all he needed. And, as I would later learn, it was built entirely with materials that he acquired either in or around the area, sometimes bartering for supplies that he could not readily obtain himself.

I had never been to a hermit's house before, so I didn't really know what to expect. Whoever this fellow was, he certainly appeared to be into working on cars, as a number of different vehicles in various stages of assembly were spread out across the front and side lawns. An engine was hoisted up in the air over the hood of an ancient pickup truck, and a pair of automobile chassis from previous eras sat quietly decaying under the tall spruce trees surrounding the house.

I walked over the soft dirt in front of the house, arriving all too quickly in front of a faded white door. Even though I hadn't made much noise, I was certain that the inhabitant knew that I was there. I knocked tentatively, waiting for the six-shooter to appear through the front window, which was slightly ajar.

For a few moments, I heard nothing but the sounds of the woods around me. Some bees buzzed around the roof of the shack, while a few songbirds called down from their lofty nests in the trees. In the background, a brook burbled away as the cool water rolled over the mossy rocks and submerged tree roots.

I was beginning to think that nobody was home, when I heard some footsteps shuffling along the floor inside the cabin. Even though the structure was rather small, they seemed to take a long time to reach the front door. Then, the door creaked open, and an elderly man stepped into view.

He stood quite straight, and looked at me from behind a pair of lively blue eyes. Although I knew he was in his seventies, he still looked in good enough physical shape to get a job on any road crew. Maybe this wouldn't be so bad after all.

"Hello, Leighton?" I asked inquiringly, even though I was certain it was him.

"Yeah," was his one word response, although he drew it out in a manner that expressed a desire to know who I was. He looked very friendly.

"My name's Larry and I'm the new trail ranger back in the West Canadas. I took over Ben Woodard's position and he went up to work in the High Peaks area around Lake Placid. He asked me to stop by and say hello."

"Well, that's nice to hear, Ben was a good man. C'mon in and I'll fix us up a cup of coffee."

As he spoke, Leighton reached out a hand in greeting. I shook it, and was quite surprised at the strength of his grip, which was threatening to crush a couple of my smaller fingers. I remember thinking to myself that I was glad that he was in his seventies, or I would have been in trouble.

Leighton's house was as modest on the inside as it appeared on the exterior. Everything was designed for functionality, with little regard for the extra frills that we take for granted in the city. At the far end of the kitchen stood an enamel coated cast iron stove that was probably as old as Leighton. A wood burning stove in the living room provided the heat for the house, while the windows and tall trees overhead provided the "air conditioning." I noticed that he did have a propane fueled refrigerator, which sat in the corner next to the sink. There was no running water inside the cabin, and the bathroom was a double-seater outhouse that was attached to the garage.

I sat down at the table in the kitchen and started talking with Leighton. It was a warm day, and the windows were open to the outside air. Leighton talked about the area, and how he came to be situated back there. Every so often, he punctuated his monologue by picking up the fly swatter and beating back some house-flies that congregated on the table.

As it turned out, he (like John Remias) was not native to the area. He had lived in town for a good part of his life, and had only moved into the woods after retiring from a career at the Remington plant near Utica.

Leighton's father, Mal, had operated a very small store along the dirt road that runs through Perkins Clearing, dispensing candy and soda through the front window of the building that also served as his house. Prior to the construction of Route 30, it had been the major road that went from Speculator to Indian Lake.

From all accounts, Leighton moved back into Perkins Clearing in the early 1970s, and took up residence in the same shelter that his father had leased from the International Paper Company. He was an avid recorder of events, and kept a daily diary in which he documented the weather, along with a listing of the vis-itors who stopped by to see him. That record was extensive, as Leighton had a lot of visitors. He was immensely popular with the local population, as well as with the owners of the various camps that had sprung up in the area. It was not uncommon to see two or three cars at a time parked out front of his building as their owners stopped by to say hello.

I stayed in Leighton's house a lot longer than I had expected that first day, getting a history lesson about the origin of the camps and roads surrounding Sled Harbor. Sled Harbor is a clear-ing a couple of miles further down the road that was used by log-gers in their local harvesting efforts. Hikers entering the woods from Perkins Clearing can now drive their vehicles right through Sled Harbor in route to the trailhead at the base of Pillsbury Mountain.

Leighton was highly intelligent, energetic, and could always find the time to brew up a good cup of coffee whenever company stopped by. He would have been impossible to dislike. It wasn't long before I developed a regular weekly routine that included a social call at Leighton's humble abode. Whenever I was scheduled to patrol the "Perkins Clearing Route," I'd stop by the bakery and pick up a coffeecake to bring along. Leighton would provide the coffee, and we'd spend an hour or two conversing on any number of topics.

He especially enjoyed antique cars, as evidenced by the proliferation of auto calendars that hung from various nails in the kitchen wall. I could show him any picture of any vehicle built over the past sixty years, and he'd instantly identify it by make, model, and year. The only problem was that he'd then pontificate about the mechanical advantages and disadvantages of its engine and inner workings, of which he appeared to know a great deal. He was a genuine enthusiast, and had an old Willys automobile in his garage which he was planning on restoring to its original salesroom condition.

Leighton's interests were extensive and diverse. Sometimes he was all work, while other times he was more interested in play. I know for a fact that he was an avid dancer, and could spin his partner with zeal down at the local dances at Graham's bar in Speculator. During several of our conversations, he spoke about some of his dancing partners with an unmistakable twinkle in his eye. I remember wishing that I'd still have that twinkle when I am his age.

In addition to dancing, Leighton would gladly take on competitors in a number of sporting events. The horseshoe pit that was laid out in front of his house invited me to make the mistake of challenging him to his own game, which was probably not very smart. I learned quite quickly that horseshoes is a game of experience, and that an old-timer could "clean your clock," so to speak, in a hurry if he felt like it. But it was fun, and we played countless rounds of the game over the next few years. As a matter of fact, one summer, I actually won a game from him. I believe that made the score 134-1.

However, I didn't know that any of this would yet take place. I was still in the process of getting acquainted with the man, and I was enjoying the conversation. Leighton showed me where to park my car so that he could keep an eye on it while I was away, and then gave me directions on how to find a few "unpublicized" springs on the way back into the West Canada Lakes. His advice struck me as being quite fatherly, and he genuinely seemed to care about my well being while hiking the trails of the territory.

Given time, I would realize that Leighton's friendly personality and caring nature were just a few of the reasons why he was so well liked in the area. When he asked you how you felt, he did so because he really wanted to know. His gentle demeanor and time-wizened philosophies have helped me from time to time over the years, and I'd like to think I've become a better person by trying to emulate him in a number of ways. However, no matter how hard I've tried, I'm still lousy at horseshoes.

—12—

Campfires

I was once discussing the topic of hikers and campers with Jerry Blake, who was one of the local old-time hunters in our neck of the woods. Jerry made biannual pilgrimages to some of the less frequently visited lakes in our region, trying to snag the prized brook trout that probably no longer existed.

The two of us were sitting on the edge of the Sampson Lake lean-to, looking out over the water. It was a quiet day. But then again, it was always quiet at Sampson Lake, as nobody ever went there. As a matter of fact, in my entire three years patrolling the area, it was one of the few occasions that I ever had company in that location.

Jerry was in his late fifties, and he had been hunting and fishing throughout the area for almost thirty years. Because of this, he was a genuine authority on the local woods and camps, and could identify where many old structures and logging tracks of the past used to be. I always enjoyed meeting up with him.

He was a fairly large man, with short gray hair that stood straight up from the top of his head. As we talked, he puffed continuously on the Camel cigarette that appeared to be permanently affixed to his lips. The lines on his weathered face deepened as he grimaced, putting the sole of his boot through a piece of kindling wood for the evening fire.

"Y'know, Larry," he said in a gravelly voice, "I can tell a lot about a person just by looking at their campfire."

His statement had a lot of truth in it, for most people in the backwoods are passionate about when and how they build their daily fire. I imagine that an inspired psychiatrist would have enjoyed doing some "pyre-analysis" on many of our visitors.

In my experience, a campfire was one of the few common bonds that tied everyone together. Almost without exception, any group found staying in the backwoods overnight would have some type of fire going. It was the centerpiece of the campsite; a source of warmth and light around which everyone would gather at day's end to eat and socialize.

I listened while Jerry reminisced about his past. "Now, my father, he could build a fire. The first thing he'd do after setting up camp was to chop down about three trees, and that would be enough just for the first day!"

I had to laugh, because I've shared lean-tos with many folks who believe that bigger is better when it comes to campfires. And I've seen some truly remarkable blazes. My thoughts wandered back into time, recalling some of the more memorable fires that I'd sat around since starting on as a park ranger.

For some reason, it was usually the older folks who tended to build the four-alarm bonfires. Maybe it was because the younger hikers never carried the saws and axes that were required to cut the bigger pieces of wood. Or possibly the younger hikers had already spent all their energy pounding along the trail that day, and were too tuckered out to build a major end-of-day blaze. But, for whatever the reason, they usually didn't.

Visitors in the West Canada Lakes area were blessed with an abundance of fuel for whatever size fire they desired to build. The predominance of hardwood trees combined with the relative lack of hikers made for a ready source of firewood within a short walking distance. I always enjoyed this advantage over some of my friends in the higher-use regions. I never could see walking a quarter-mile to bring back a couple of scrawny sticks. But I did enjoy having a small nightly fire, as I greatly preferred cooking over that than a gas stove.

Personally, I've always subscribed to the "Two-Inch Theory," which says that if the branch is over two inches in diameter, I really don't need it. It's too heavy to carry, and the chances are pretty good that I won't be able to use my knee to break it into fire-place-sized lengths. And, as any lightweight-minded hiker knows, God gave man the knee for the sole purpose of breaking firewood.

Wood selection was another way in which I could discriminate the woodsmen from the first-time visitors. For as any experienced fire builder knows, there are certain types of wood that are absolutely useless for burning.

Over-enthusiastic individuals would stop at nothing to build their woodpile. The fact that a tree was still standing meant nothing to them. Illegal as it was, we'd often come across fresh piles of sawdust next to a newly exposed stump. This tended to expand the clear-cut areas around the lean-tos on a continuous basis.

In general, coniferous wood never burns as well as hardwoods, such as beech or maple. Many times, the larger pieces wouldn't burn at all, as they may still have been alive when the damn fools cut them down. Every lean-to had a few of these inflammable mementos gracing their fireplaces.

On other occasions, I've seen groups of pyromaniacs get real barnburner blazes going, only to have the spruce logs arrange their own Fourth of July fireworks. This happens when the sap pockets in the wood start to heat up and explode, which sends wonderfully hot glowing briquettes flying in random directions around the fire. I once saw one of these rockets land directly in the middle of a fellow's cup of coffee. Believe it or not, that didn't stop him from finishing his drink; he claimed that "it heated it up for me, but gave it a rather smoky taste!"

Yeah, I guess Jerry was right. Everyone had their own ideas on how to build a fire, and you could tell a lot about them just from watching.

I sat and watched my companion as he knelt in front of the fireplace grates. He was stoking the six-inch flames with some maple twigs that he found within thirty feet of the lean-to.

"That's all she needs to cook this up. Let's leave the bigger stuff for the next group that comes through."

Like most good woodsmen, he stashed a pile of kindling wood and some nice dry beech branches underneath the sheltered roof of the lean-to, just enough for the next group (who might arrive in the rain) to get a warm fire going.

It was getting dark, and we prepared to turn in for the night. Jerry placed a few larger limbs on the fire, which would give us enough light to take care of our final chores before night fell. As the branches caught fire, the orange flames rose above the bricks of the fireplace, blending nicely with the fading crimson colors of the sunset sky.

From the warmth of my sleeping bag I watched the decreasing light cast longer and longer shadows against the lean-to and the flicker of the flames slowly die out.

—13—

Simon's Midnight Madness

"Simon Schute; Party of 1; Oneonta, New York; Northville to Lake Placid."

The penciled-in line in the Piseco register booth looked common enough. After all, we had many solo hikers who were doing the entire trail that summer. I had spoken with quite a few of them at the various campsites and lean-tos, and had discovered that many of these individuals had hiked by themselves for years.

I don't believe in stereotyping people, as everyone is different. However, one trait that I found shared by the majority of these lone hikers was their tendency towards introversion. They were all quite friendly, mind you, but they tended to listen to me talk rather than initiate a conversation themselves.

And then there was Simon.

I got my first glimpse of the gentlemen as I was approaching the South Lake lean-to that sunny September afternoon. It was warmer than most September days, with the blue sky reflecting clearly off the shallow, sandy-bottomed lake. South Lake was the only location in our entire wilderness area that boasted a white sand beach, which made it a popular stopping point on the trail.

What I first saw puzzled me a bit. The fellow looked old. Quite old. He was wearing a long red coat that looked as though it was filled with goose down, which was quite incongruous with the afternoon heat. His long gray hair spilled over the collar of the coat and continued approximately eight inches down his back.

As I approached the front of the campsite, he turned around to offer greetings. And that's when I got an even greater surprise. Below an aged, smile-creased face hung the longest beard that I had ever seen in my life. It was snow white in color, and flowed in waves to a tapered point which approached his belt buckle. It had to be seen to be believed.

"Uh oh, I ain't done nothin' wrong, have I?" he asked jokingly, looking at my uniform. "'Cause if I did, I don't think I could outrun ye!"

"I don't know," I responded with a laugh, "you look darned sprightly to me. What's your time in the twenty-mile dash?"

The senior citizen cut loose with a roar of laughter. "Better than it was five years ago, I reckon. I'm retired for a few years now, and I'm still tryin' to make up for sittin' on my duff behind the steering wheel of a bus for half my life."

He introduced himself to me as Simon Schute, a retiree from Oneonta, New York. From the time I had seen his name in the register booth I had wanted to meet him, since I attended college in Oneonta. I just hadn't expected a Rip Van Winkle look-alike.

"You know, you've got one of the finest lean-tos in the entire region all to yourself," I said, looking around the empty structure. "And it's such a nice clear night to spend here; there should be a lot of stars out. I'm half-tempted to leave my pack here, finish my patrol, and camp here tonight."

Simon nodded his head vigorously. "Sure, I'd welcome the company. It got a bit lonely the last couple of nights down south of here. I pitched a tent over by the Jessup River on Friday night, and then stayed by myself at the second Spruce Lake lean-to last night. Not another soul in sight. Kind of quiet when there's nobody else around to talk to."

And Simon apparently enjoyed a bit of conversation, because he could speak on a wide variety of subjects. As a matter of fact, I soon became aware that I couldn't get much of a word in edge-wise. And I consider myself to be quite a talker.

It was after 3:00 P.M. by the time I managed to extricate my-self from Simon's monologues. I had been truly enjoying the dis-cussion, which ranged from rugby to the fine points of carving a Meerschaum pipe. But if I was to complete my six-mile, round-trip patrol to Sampson Lake and back in time for dinner, I'd have to hustle.

I can still recall how beautiful the trees looked on that early fall afternoon as I hurried along the seldom-used trail. The leaves were starting to turn color, and the red maples were already showing some of their characteristic bright crimson hues.

What a day! It was a pleasure to hike almost anywhere with-out my entire seventy pound pack along for the ride. Without all that weight, I could sometimes average four miles an hour with-out really rushing my steps. And before I knew it, I was rounding the final curve in the trail and returning to South Lake. The round trip had taken less than two hours.

"What's the matter," I asked, "don't like the way I keep house?"

Simon looked up from his work, and then glanced quickly at his watch. "Well, I hadn't expected to see you back here so soon. You must 'a done a bit of quick steppin'."

"No, not really. The trail's in pretty good shape, and there was nobody to talk with over at Sampson." I reverted to the subject of accommodations. "Hey, there's plenty of room over in the lean-to. And we hardly ever get mosquitoes bothering us this late in the year. Why are you bothering to pitch a tent?"

"Oh, just a small problem I've got," replied Simon. He leaned back on his heels and tugged reflectively on his beard. "Ye see, I've been told that I snore a bit. I ain't sure whether I really believe that or not, but I don't like to think that I'm bothering anybody. So I try and put a little distance between me and the other hikers at night."

I looked at him with an ever widening grin that quickly progressed into a chuckle, and then into a belly whopper of a laugh. "Get out of here! You're joking! Nobody sets up their tent that far away because they snore."

"No I'm serious," answered the old-timer. "Back before my wife passed away, we'd have to get separate rooms at the motel when we went on vacation. She'd say that she'd rather sleep inside a jet engine than in the same room with me. I guess I get rather loud, but then again, I'm never awake to hear it!"

I felt a bit embarrassed, as I was laughing so hard that I had tears running down my face. I accepted his explanations, although with more than a trace of doubt. How could anyone be that loud?

We went about our activities around the evening fire, which Simon enlivened with his constant banter. In between discourses, he prepared one of the most unusual dishes that I had ever seen cooked in the backwoods, peanut chili. It contained dried beef, peanuts, peppers, and a delicious curry chili sauce that he simmered slowly over the coals.

Simon wanted to share this delicacy with me. He seemed to want to share everything, not the least of which was his accumulated wit and wisdom. He was a lot of fun to be with, and I thought it was odd that he had chosen to walk to Lake Placid by himself. Surely, a man of his temperament would have enjoyed company along the way.

Soon it was dusk, and I rolled my sleeping bag out across the lean-to floor. It had been a pleasant evening, with the wind remaining fairly calm and the temperature hovering in the seventies. Not bad at all. In fact, I remember thinking to myself that it would be a perfect night for sleeping.

I bid Simon goodnight as he wandered off towards his tent. He was still wearing the bulky red coat that I had first seen him in. I wondered if he slept in it as well.

The night air was cool, and I quickly drifted off to sleep, lost in my own dreams. I was dreaming about trying to build a cabin, but was getting frustrated. The darned chainsaw wouldn't start. I kept pulling on the cord, harder and harder, but I just couldn't get it going. With each pull, the engine redoubled its efforts to catch, but to no avail.

I had never had a dream like this before. The engine noise increased with each attempt, while I perspired from the exertion. I was breathing harder and harder, while the saw was getting louder and louder. I just had to get it to work. It was getting too noisy—too loud! Stop pulling! Stop the noise! Stop the noise!

I awoke in a sweat. Realizing that I was breathing hard, I pulled the sleeping bag off of me, allowing the cool night air to flow over my body. What a dream!

But wait! Was I still dreaming? For in the background, I heard the roar of the chainsaw, now even louder than before. It seemed to echo in pulses, which then bounced around the inside walls of the lean-to. This was impossible; I was awake.

I scrambled from my sleeping bag and tossed on my boots. They felt cold on my feet. I remember thinking that my feet had never felt cold in a dream before, so I must've been awake.

By the time I lunged out of the lean-to, the loons out on the lake were responding to the noise with some calls of their own. They were a half-mile away!

I grabbed the flashlight and pointed it towards the source of the ruckus, which was along the trail leading away from the lean-to. And there, in the distant beam of the light, lay Simon's tent.

Amazing! I approached the structure with awe. How could any living thing make that much noise without awakening itself? There were great, thundering rumbles, which were interspersed with whining, whistling exhalation sounds. I had never heard anything like that in my life. And though I couldn't expect anyone to believe it, I actually witnessed the strings that held up the tent vibrating in the night air. Wow!

Well, the mystery had been solved, and I was eventually able to get back to sleep. It was a bit of a restless sleep though, as I dreamt of locomotives, diesel engines, and volcanoes.

The following morning I awoke quite early, still feeling as though I hadn't been to bed yet. I decided to take a quick run up to see John at the caretakers' cabin on West Lake. It was only a short hike from South Lake, about a half-mile away.

Simon was just getting up when I returned. He crawled from his tent while pulling the zipper up on his red jacket. He stretched, yawned a big yawn, and asked, "How'd you sleep?"

I looked back at him, trying to figure out just how to answer that one. How could I tell him? Was it possible that he didn't know?

"Fine, Simon, just fine," I lied. "Great night for sleeping."

I don't think he would have believed me anyway.

—14—

Practical Jokes

I've always had a peculiar sense of humor which has, on occasion, gotten me into trouble. It's never been my large supply of bad jokes that's been the culprit, but rather the infrequent practical joke that I've enjoyed playing on my friends and co-workers.

Don't misunderstand, I've never approved of doing anything that causes damage to property, or that will hurt anyone's feelings. But I've always had a soft spot for whoopee cushions and garlic flavored chewing gum. I just can't seem to help it.

But this entire episode, strange as it may seem, was not of my doing. (Well, at least I didn't start it!) It was John Remias' own brand of humor, perhaps born out of boredom, which caused him to draw first blood. From then on, it was war. I was merely a willing participant.

Funny as it was, I never suspected a thing. I was heading north from West Canada Creek, in route to my final destination of Cedar Lakes. It was a cool day in August, and I wanted to stop by John's cabin for a chat. I took off my pack on the front porch and propped it up against a chair.

As I opened the front door screen, I found John perched on a step ladder. He was changing a strip of flypaper that hung from one of the beams in the middle of the living room. John tended to do this only on rare occasions, usually after the used strip had entrapped its limit of carcasses. It was not a pretty sight.

"Hey Mr. Park Ranger!" he cackled with one of his wide grins. "Stayin' away from the hikers today, or did they catch up to ya?"

John invited me into the cabin to talk for a while, which I always enjoyed; I found John's unique conversational mixture of anecdotes, politics, and woodland yore to be irresistible.

I was about ready to flop into a comfortable looking rocking chair when John asked me to check on the second West Lake lean-to, which was about two hundred yards up the trail from his cabin. It was a bit unusual, as he had never asked me to do this before, but anything for a friend, right?

The trip to the lean-to took about five minutes, after which I retraced my steps and reentered the cabin. John had finished replacing the fly traps, and had poured coffee for both of us.

As always, we talked for way too long, and it was mid-afternoon by the time I noticed that I was behind schedule. That often happened at John's cabin. Then again, there was never any rush back there, as long as we covered our assigned route for the day. If I hustled, I'd make it to Cedar Lakes by 5:30 P.M.

Heaving my pack onto my back, I knew that I'd been sitting down too long. My legs must have fallen asleep, as the pack felt heavier than usual. But no matter, it was time to go, and I still had six miles to cover before setting up camp.

I'm not sure when the fatigue started setting in for real, but somewhere between Cat Lake and King's Pond my body started to complain. Was I getting out of shape? I thought that I was in pretty good condition, with all that hiking around the area with my oversized Kelty pack. Yet, as I trudged on towards Cedar Lakes, I was really feeling it. My legs didn't have the spring that I was used to, and my back felt as though it was carrying a dump truck. I was not feeling well.

Instead of two and a half hours to Cedar Lakes, the trip took over three hours, and I'd about had it. I gladly slipped my pack off, allowing it to drop heavily on the ground in front of the lean-to by the dam. I leaned back to stretch, feeling the sweat pour down the inside of my shirt. Maybe I was sick? Well, it would do me no good to stand around the lean-to feeling sorry for myself. I might as well get unpacked, and then start dinner.

As I loosened the cords from the top of the pack, I noticed that everything was "riding high," with some of my belongings hanging over the top rim of the nylon compartment. And as I unpacked, I observed that several items had shifted position inside the pack, which I never experienced before. But besides that, everything else was normal, and nothing was out of place.

Until I came to the rocks.

The first one was small, about the size of a tennis ball. It was concealed innocently enough, buried beneath my two quart cook-pot. I must admit that, at first, I thought it might have been an accidental packing, until I found the second rock concealed inside an arm of my wool jacket.

From then on, they got progressively larger, with some of the boulders at the bottom reaching truly impressive sizes. I unloaded them onto the front of the lean-to, deciding that I'd use them to rebuild part of the disintegrating fireplace.

Thanks, John! So that's way he'd wanted me to check the lean-to. I should have known.

I remember laughing while swearing under my breath at the same time. Ok, two could play at this game! After all, John had started something here, and it was up to me to make him pay.

The month that followed was a constant battle of wits; a chess match was being played out between John's cabin and my tent. It was my move. So on my next pass by the West Canadas station, I stopped and went into John's outhouse. With me, I had the pint of spruce gum sap that I'd been collecting all week long.

It's amazing how long it takes to spread spruce sap evenly

onto an outhouse seat, especially if you want to spread it thinly, so that the next unwary user will not detect the substance before sitting on it. It took me almost twenty minutes with a shoe polishing brush, dipping and rubbing, until every square inch of the "throne" was covered. Then, I hid behind a shed and waited for my quarry.

I hadn't long to wait, as John had just finished working on the phone line east of the cabin and was returning for his lunch. He dropped his tools on the porch and stumped over to the outhouse without suspecting a thing. I remained hidden, barely holding back my laughter. By golly, I had him!

The torrent of four-letter words that poured from the outhouse window was proof enough of my success. John was in rare form, and there was no doubt in my mind that he knew who the perpetrator was. The only problem was that he could not get out of the outhouse soon enough to catch me, as he was firmly attached to the seat for a good five minutes. I took off at a gallop, laughing all the way back to Cedar Lakes.

I was still chuckling at the thought of my brilliant victory two weeks later, as I sat in the outhouse by the Beaver Pond lean-to. (Outhouses seem to make good settings for this type of humor.) I had won, and John had been defeated. Score one for me!

My laughter was shut-off completely as I pulled my "music roll" (toilet paper) from its stuff sack. There it sat, encased in its plastic bag, and covered with one of the thickest layers of molasses I had ever seen. Oh, hell. This was war.

I knew that John never used an alarm clock to get up in the morning. He just slept until the sun came up. Not that anyone would have known if he overslept, as we were so many miles away from anywhere, but John was most diligent in his efforts, and was always on the job quite early in the morning.

The sunlight that provided John with his morning wake-up call came through two small windows in his bedroom. I knew that they'd be my next target.

It was a Sunday night when I snuck into the clearing on West

Lake that surrounds the log cabin. The clock read only 9:15 P.M., but John had already turned out the lights and retired for the evening. Perfect! I removed the roll of black crepe paper and package of thumb tacks from my pack. I used these to completely cover the two window frames.

Then, I grabbed several sheets of the roofing tarpaper that I had already positioned in the woods nearby. Silently, I leaned the sheets up against the inside of the sills, adding yet another layer of light-blocking material to the pile. Then, I sat back and inspected my work. Yes! That should do the trick.

It was almost noon the next day when the pair of hikers knocked on John's door. They looked like a young married couple, full of energy and ambition. They must have gotten an early start, as they'd already covered the seven miles from their previous bivouac at Pillsbury Lake.

There was a long pause after their first attempt, while they both stood looking expectantly at the closed door. The young man then tried again, rapping a bit louder on the hardwood surface. "Hello, Hello?" he called, as though willing someone to appear. "Anybody home?"

After a lengthy delay, the front door opened slowly. From my position behind the chimney in the front yard I could see John, who was dressed in a pair of blue pajamas. He was blinking the light out of his eyes while looking suspiciously up at the sun. Meanwhile, the female hiker did a double-take, glancing at her watch before looking at John's pajamas.

Yes! Score: John—2, Larry—2. It was now a tie.

As I think back on the whole thing, that was definitely my best prank. Even John appreciated the effort, saying that he'd awakened several times, thinking that it seemed like a rather long night. I felt good, as I'd pulled off a real masterpiece. John seemed willing to agree to a ceasefire, so that would be the end of our duel.

I ate lunch in the cabin with John, and then prepared to leave for my patrol to Cedar River Flow, about eleven miles away. John walked out front with me, and smiled as I hoisted my pack onto my back.

Uh oh. It felt heavy again.

I turned to face my tormentor, who looked like a spider waiting to pounce on a fly ensnared in its web. "Thanks, John. How many rocks did you put in my pack today?"

"I didn't put any rocks in there," he responded with a slightly hurt expression. "I already used that one on you. I'd never pull the same trick twice."

"Darn it, John," I yelled, "I think you've given me another part of your rock garden. This thing feels ten pounds heavier than it did an hour ago."

"Larry, I promise. I swear on the Bible, I didn't put any rocks in your pack. You have my word on it."

I looked at him with a level stare. John had never lied to me about anything, and I knew that he was true to his word. Maybe the pack just felt heavy. Anyway, I really didn't feel like unpacking it to check, so I said goodbye and left for my patrol.

It was almost four hours later when I huffed into the lean-to at Cedar River Flow. My back was tired once again, and I was once again suspicious. I unpacked quickly, expecting the worst.

Well, at least John had been telling me the truth back there at the station. As promised, there was not a rock to be found anywhere. As a matter of fact, John couldn't have put any rocks inside my pack that day, because there just wasn't any spare room to put them. John's old horseshoe set took up every square inch of available space.

To the best of my knowledge, the lean-to at Cedar River Flow remains as the only remote campsite in the Adirondack Park complete with its own official weight horseshoe set.

Final score: John—3, Larry—2.

—15—

Blending In

I'm not really sure when it began, or when I first noticed it. It just somehow happened when I wasn't paying attention.

John Giedraitis had often spoken about the phenomenon of blending into the surroundings, becoming used to the environment in the backcountry. "It'll take a while," he said of the transition. "For the first month or two you'll miss a lot. Your ears will be used to the noise of the city, and they'll act like filters. But once you get used to being back there, you'll actually hear a lot more of what's going on around you. It'll surprise you."

At first, I didn't know whether to believe John or not. It all sounded too existential for me, and I'm normally quite the realist. After all, I thought, why should one month be different from the next? I'd still be walking down the same trails, surrounded by the same woods, and listening to the same creatures.

I had always known about physical acclimatization, which involves getting your body used to new environments. It is similar to high-altitude climbers who stay at a certain level for a day or two before proceeding upward. Yet it is different. This involved a whole new mindset, and I just couldn't imagine it.

It wasn't until almost three months into my first year as a wilderness ranger that I realized a change had indeed occurred. I was walking along the northern shore of West Canada Lake on an overcast July morning. It was one of those days when the air was perfectly still, without as much as a ripple on the lake. The sky was covered with a blanket of grayish-white clouds which occasionally spilled a few raindrops through the canopy of trees overhead. Not really thick clouds, like the cumulus nimbus "thunderheads," but rain clouds nonetheless.

As I strolled along the path, I realized that things were, well, different than they'd been when I started on the job. I was beginning to notice so much more of what was going on around me, while I was less consciously thinking about it.

Perhaps it was the familiarity with my surroundings that was causing the change. Sort of like moving into a new office building; you've got to learn where everything is located before really feeling comfortable. But somehow, it was deeper than that. After all, it had taken me just a few short weeks to learn the trail systems, and then perhaps an additional month to become intimately familiar with the hills, lakes, and streams of the area.

No, this was something else. This was a mental adjustment which allowed me to finally become part of the mosaic. I found myself acting more on instinct and less on conscious decisions. I also became aware of specific sounds (or lack of them) that I never could've imagined before.

The families of red squirrels that live in that beech tree; I wonder where they are today? There's that same brook trout splashing about down by the big rock. He's a bit early today. The mother Great Blue Heron is still sitting on her nest. I guess her eggs haven't hatched yet. Where's that loon's mate? She never comes down here by herself. The sun is almost two fists above Cobble Hill, it must be about five minutes to nine.

The feeling of being totally in sync with the woods and its inhabitants is an incredible experience that cannot be fully appreciated without living it for oneself. On a personal level, it provided me with a great amount of satisfaction and peace. Many of the small concerns that I previously had in my life, faded into insignificance.

The weather was a good example of this phenomenon. Rain used to bother me as I slogged through the streets of Syracuse, cursing at the precipitation. But within a few months of taking up residence in the back woods, it just didn't matter. Rain, fog, sun, it was all the same to me. It was just the weather, and I was happy to go with the flow.

I also became familiar with the individual creatures that surrounded me on a daily basis. After a while, you just know when a particular loon is going to call, or when your favorite chipmunk is going to stop by for a snack. You become acquainted with them, and they become your friends, which can also lead to the chipmunk helping himself to your entire weekly supply of peanuts! It all becomes part of the scheme.

Perhaps the epitome of this phenomenon happened to me one night during a storm at the Beaver Pond lean-to. The clouds had been thickening all day long, and were truly menacing by the time early evening arrived. The wind had been increasing in velocity at a steady rate, and was forming whitecaps on the normally calm pond. I ate dinner in an eerie premature darkness that was a premonition of the ominous strength of the approaching storm.

I climbed into my sleeping bag in pitch blackness, as the wind had actually blown out my small cooking fire. In the darkness, I heard the rumbles of distant thunder, growing louder by the minute. This would be one for the books. The lightening bolts began to shoot over the hills along the southern edge of Cedar Lakes, lighting up the sky with their bright blue brilliance.

I lay back in the lean-to, feeling the wind picking up spray off the pond. It was the only time that I had ever seen that happen. I was being treated to a natural laser show, and I had the theater all to myself. Or so I thought.

I heard a few noises filtering down from above me, coming from the top beam of the lean-to. Turning over in my sleeping bag, I realized that the tree swallows that had built a nest up there were camped directly above me, and were settling in for the evening. I imagined that they were probably looking down at me while I was looking up at them.

As the wind increased to a veritable gale, I heard the sounds of tree limbs breaking and branches snapping. The rain was falling in sheets, which were being driven into the front of the lean-to. I moved my sleeping bag back up against the logs of the rear wall to take advantage of the overhanging roof. At one time, this sort of thing would have bothered me. But that night, I just sat and watched and listened in awe as the storm continued to intensify.

One of the mice that normally tip-toed around the lean-to in search of food had decidedly seen enough, and jumped frantically through the zipper into my sleeping bag. I was about to push him out when I decided otherwise. He wasn't doing anything but getting out of the wind and rain, so I let him stay. Within a few minutes he had curled in a ball against my shoulder and had gone to sleep.

One other animal joined us in the shelter that night. It landed on the floor of the lean-to in full stride, as though it was sprinting towards a finish line and then jumped inside. I was partially asleep by that time, and never got a good look at it. About all I can say is that it was bigger than a squirrel but smaller than a beaver.

But no matter, there was plenty of room for anything that wanted to come inside. Maybe it was just my imagination, but I felt a strange camaraderie with the other huddled residents of the lean-to on that most unusual night. There was no need for rules or protocol. We were all the same that night, just creatures under one roof, taking shelter from a storm.

The Streaker

The name in the Cedar Lakes register booth read "Ross R. Braggs," and he was en route from Blue Mountain Lake to Northville. Many people did selected portions of the Placid Trail like that, so there was no reason to suspect anything suspicious about this fellow. I noticed that he was a party of "1," and that he had passed by the register booth the day before. No further entries had been recorded since his.

I arrived at the Beaver Pond lean-to quite late in the day, and immediately began my evening preparations. The lean-to was clean, although there was something hanging from a nail in the back corner of the structure.

"Oh great," I thought to myself, "another wet sweatshirt that someone didn't feel like carrying out of the woods." Unfortunately, this was a common occurrence; useless pieces of dirty, wet clothing would get left behind, only to lie rotting forever in a garbage pile behind the lean-to. On more than one occasion, I had burned articles of clothing that had dried sufficiently to ignite. Why didn't people just think before they did something like that?

I climbed up under the roof and pulled down the garment, which to my surprise felt warm and soft. Examining the label, I discovered that it was a Johnson wool shirt, which is a premium brand of outerwear. It looked to be fairly new, and without any real signs of wear. And it was my size!

As I looked over the rugged shirt, a note fell from one of the upper pockets. It was neatly printed in ink, and simply read: "No room in my pack—I'm trying to lighten my load. If it fits you, it's yours!" It was signed "Ross R. Braggs."

Well thank you, Mr. Braggs! Gifts like this didn't usually just show up in lean-tos, and I put the shirt into my pack.

The following morning, I set off toward the West Canadas at a leisurely pace. I made it to the end of Cedar Lakes, and then left the trail in order to detour towards the Third Cedar Lake lean-to. It was a deserted spot about a half-mile off of the Placid Trail, and was seldom frequented by anyone but the local fishermen.

As I suspected, there were no campers there, and the lean-to was completely empty. Well, almost. In the front of the lean-to, tucked neatly away into a corner, were several camping items that someone had left behind. They included some canned goods, two shiny new camp plates with silverware, a guide book to the Northville-Lake Placid Trail, and a collection of T-shirts. And once again, a note from Ross R. Braggs, offering these personal belongings to anyone who wanted to carry them out of the woods.

I must admit that, although this was littering, I still got a chuckle out of the whole thing. After all, here was this poor soul who was so burdened by his load that he was leaving behind his clothing as he went.

I made it down to West Lake later on that morning. That's when I popped my head into the lean-to south of John's cabin and saw the brand new pair of quality leather hiking boots sitting there in the corner. They were a well known brand, and the rich leather uppers indicated the expensive price tag that they had probably carried just a short time earlier.

Once again, a neatly written note accompanied the boots.

"These boots are really nice, but they're too new. I've got blis-ters on top of my blisters, and I just can't wear them anymore. I'm switching to my sneakers, so anyone who could use a good pair of size "10s" is more than welcome to this pair."

Size ten? That's my size! Once again, my pack opened up and absorbed another piece of gear. My pack was growing heavier with each new acquisition, although I really didn't care. A pair of boots like that would have set me back almost a week's pay, and I wasn't going to let the opportunity pass. Especially since the pair that I had on was showing signs of "giving up the ghost" in the near future.

I stopped at John's cabin on West Lake to talk for a while. John said that he'd been in for part of the morning, but hadn't seen anyone pass by. And yet, Mr. Braggs had definitely been there, as he had already signed the register in back of John's cabin. The date next to his signature indicated that he'd passed through earlier that morning. I was getting more curious with each passing hour.

"C'mon, John, surely you must have seen him go by?" I asked. "He'd be hard to miss, he's the one without shoes or a shirt! I'm going to follow him south, just in case he decides to ditch his pack."

John was amused, and agreed on my strategy. "If I'd known that he was givin' stuff away, I'd have followed him down the trail, too," John laughed. "But hell, haven't you got enough to carry around in that rig of yours already, without having to carry someone else's stuff too?"

Nope. Not when you're dealing with that kind of merchandise. Although I still hadn't met Ross R. Braggs, one thing was very clear: he appreciated the finer things in life. Everything that he'd left behind was "top-shelf," and I was planning on getting as much of it as I could lay my hands on.

After talking with John for an hour or so, I left West Lake to continue my patrol southward towards West Canada Creek. I remember feeling a bit like a predator stalking his prey, waiting to pounce upon whatever choice items Mr. Braggs left behind.

I didn't have long to wait. The very next lean-to, on South Lake, contained the largest parcel of all. Hanging from the top wooden beam was a very fancy day pack, which was stuffed to the gills with food and drink mixes. The shelf of the lean-to held what looked to be a new camp stove, which was accompanied by a set of cooking bowls and handles. Sitting on the floor of the structure was a variety of additional clothing that must have been jettisoned within the past hour or so.

It was a virtual shopping mall. I removed my pack and stepped up into the shelter in order to further examine the stuff. Then, I looked around the lean-to for the now familiar note, which I located tucked away beneath the stove on the shelf.

Reading the note, I quickly realized why Mr. Braggs had decided to rid himself of so much ballast at this particular spot; he had "had it," and was hightailing it out of the woods via Perkins Clearing. For reasons unknown to me, he had decided that it was not in his best interest to continue all the way to Northville. This would be the end of the road for his trek.

I was saddened as I realized that this load was the grand finale, and that my good luck had come to an end. I decided to keep the stove and the day pack, which I still use to this day. I was tempted to keep the cooking pots as well, until I reminded myself that I'd first have to find room in my pack, which was now bursting at the seams.

I also inventoried the clothing, which included a few additional surprises. Folded neatly into the stack were two pairs of bright cotton hiking shorts, woolen socks, and a stack of underwear. Underwear? Just what was this fellow wearing by now, anyway? Over the past two days, I'd recovered his shirts, pants, socks, and undergarments. For his sake, I hoped that he had at least one additional outfit in his pack. Otherwise, the mosquitoes could have made his final walk out to Perkins Clearing extremely uncomfortable!

Much to my chagrin, I never did get to meet Ross R. Braggs, even though I still do own quite a bit of his stuff. He evidently made it out of the woods, as I found his name logged into the registration booth outside of Perkins Clearing. He had signed out two days earlier, and then probably hitched a ride into the town of Speculator, hopefully stopping at a clothing store.

I'll never forget the final remarks that Mr. Braggs jotted down in our ledger book as he was leaving the woods. Short and to the point, they probably summed up the feelings that many of our visitors have after a week in the West Canada Lakes. They simply read:

"Too many bugs. Too much rain. Too many blisters. Too heavy a pack. Had a great time. I'll be back next year!"

—17—

Born Adirondack

The people of the Adirondacks have a wonderful pride of their land that tends to come through in almost everything they say and do. In many cases, I must admit that they are a lot more educated in the "ways of the outdoors" than many folks.

The phrase, "I know, because I was born here," has always fascinated me. I was never able to determine just how some of that knowledge is passed down through the chromosomes, but evidently, it is. They swear to it!

I remember sitting in John's cabin one fall afternoon, listening to him try to explain the phenomenon. "Y'know, Larry," he winced, as the smoke from his cigarette swirled above his head, "I've been living here almost all of my life, but I'll never be accepted as a native, 'cause I wasn't born here, I was carried in." Now the girls [referring to his three daughters], they'll be accepted as local stock, as they were born after Barb and I moved here. It doesn't figure, does it?"

No, I thought, it really doesn't. Here I was, sitting in front of a man who could run rings around anyone else I knew in the woods, and he wasn't accepted as a true native because of the city listed on his birth certificate.

Now, most of the local campers who stayed in the West Canadas had passed through the area on dozens of previous occasions, and many of them knew the locations of the "other trails" that wound their way through our region. These included the hunting paths, some of the older trails and roads that used to exist before maintenance was stopped, as well as some of the original trail routes prior to re-routing. On several of these unmarked paths, it would be possible to hike for weeks on end without ever running into another human being.

This is what made these trails so appealing to some of the local hikers and hunters. It is somewhat "neat" to be able to hike around all the traffic on the Northville-Lake Placid Trail without them ever knowing that you're there. However, I very seldom followed these alternate routes, as my job involved meeting as much of the public as possible.

And then, every once in a while, I'd meet up with one of those "I know more than you" folks who claimed that they used no trails at all; folks who claimed that they walked fifteen miles through the underbrush and thicket and arrived at their precise destination without the slightest of errors. And they were able to do this, no doubt, because they were born in the Adirondacks.

One of the more interesting cases I encountered happened while I was stationed on top of Pillsbury Mountain during the fall of 1979. I was sitting up in the tower, as it was one of those few clear days that the tower was not encased in clouds. I truly loved those crisp, sunny afternoons, when you could look out over the September foliage as it turned color before your very eyes. The vision was unobstructed for over forty miles in some directions, and it felt like you could see forever.

Suddenly, my attention was directed downward, as I noticed a lone hiker emerging into the clearing in front of my cabin. The rifle slung over his shoulder attested to the fact that he was a hunter, although this was a bit unusual, as very few hunters ever climbed up to the top of the mountain in pursuit of game. He seemed to be in no particular hurry to come up the tower, as he slowly stretched and drank from a metal flask.

He also appeared to have no interest in the sign-in register that I had put up in front of the cabin. (I did this mainly for the younger visitors, who enjoyed the "I climbed Pillsbury Mountain" cards that I kept stocked there.)

Finally, after about ten minutes or so, I heard the distinct "clump-clump" of his boots as they thudded up the planked stairs. It was eight full flights to the top, so my visitor was a bit winded when he pushed up the trap door that constituted the floor of my tower enclosure.

"Hi! Welcome to Pillsbury Mountain!" I exclaimed as he lowered the door behind him. "Have a nice climb today?"

The stranger didn't respond to my remarks immediately, although I thought I discerned a slight nod of his head in acknowledgement. Instead, he looked around him as though he was inspecting his backyard for groundhog holes. Then, he took another drink from his flask, turned towards me, and started to speak.

"How long have you been up here?" he started, without preamble. It sounded like more of an accusation than a question.

"Well, I've only been up here for the past few weeks," I replied. "They pulled me out of my job as the Wilderness Park Ranger in the West Canadas so that they could have someone up here through hunting season."

"Wilderness? Ha!" he hollered. "There ain't no wilderness out there. That's just a title that the DEC gives it so that they can control what we can and can't do here. That land's no more wild than my tomato patch!"

OK. This would be an interesting discussion, although I wasn't certain that I was really up to the task of arguing with him, it was too nice of a day. So instead, I relaxed and nodded my head while my visitor relayed a steady stream of facts designed to prove his knowledge of the area.

His name was Jerry, and he was a lifetime resident of Weavertown, located southeast of Speculator. He knew all about the new trails, the old trails, the camps, the lakes, and the people. Apparently, there wasn't much of anything that Jerry didn't know about the region, as he proceeded to talk for an hour or two about a wide variety of topics. And as I mentioned, I never really challenged him on anything in particular, as I was feeling rather lazy.

It must have been about four in the afternoon before Jerry decided that he'd impressed me enough, and announced that he was leaving.

"Well, I think I'd best be heading off, before somebody else gets lucky and nails my buck," he said as he started lifting the stairwell door up. "Although I doubt that anyone ever hunts the same part of the woods that I do. Most of the city boys are afraid of going more than a couple hundred yards from the road. That's why I never use the trails."

"Just be careful," I warned him. "You get hurt too far from help, and nobody'll ever find you."

"Don't you worry yourself about that, young man," he retorted. "I can handle myself back here no matter what comes my way. I've been in these woods since I was carried in!" And with that, he ducked below the floor of the tower and started back down the stairs.

For a few minutes I watched him through the windows of my enclosure as he reached the ground and walked past my cabin. Then, to my surprise, instead of heading towards the trail, he turned west and disappeared into the woods. To my knowledge, there were no trails on that side of the mountain, not even any old or abandoned paths extended in that direction. Wow! He really must have known the area if he was heading down Pillsbury from that side.

Soon after Jerry's departure, I signed off the radio for the day and went down to the cabin for dinner. The beautiful day turned into a beautiful evening, and I ate my supper on the makeshift table that I had set out on the front porch. I always loved to do that when the weather cooperated, as I got to watch the colors of the sky turn a crimson red over the distant West Lake. Every once in a while, a flock of geese would fly directly overhead, honking loudly as they beat the air with their wings. It was a wonderful night.

The following morning was no different from any other, outside of the fact that my radio was squawking a bit more than usual. I used the propane stove to poach a few eggs, which I placed on toast slices along with some of the fake bacon that I'd carried up the week before. It came from a can, and really didn't bear too much of a resemblance to the genuine article. Breakfast assembled, I sat down at the table in the front room and started to read the latest L.L. Bean catalog.

As I started to eat, my ears began to perk up towards the radio, which was sitting on the other side of the room. I wasn't officially "on duty" until 8:00 A.M., which was when I normally turned up the volume and carried the radio up the tower. But even on low, I could hear bits and pieces of the conversation. It sounded like a search.

I moved across the room and turned up the volume so as to hear the details. Naturally, I was just plain curious to learn what was happening "down there." But I also knew that searches often included the fire tower observers, as their elevation and centralized locations made for excellent radio relay stations between the various search units.

"The subject had on a red jacket and green pants," the voice on the radio crackled. "He was armed with a .308 Winchester, and had a small brown sack with him."

Additional details continued to come in as I moved up to the tower. I still hadn't heard much about the search, and didn't know where the individual was lost. But I had to head up towards the tower anyway, and perhaps, if the search was nearby, I'd be able to see smoke from a signal fire somewhere. I knew that there wasn't much chance of this happening, but I still figured that I'd look.

Reaching the top of the tower, I looked at the skies around me. Not quite as clear as the previous day, with fog covering up some of the lower ground, but all in all, not a bad day. I plugged the radio into the tower's jack and settled into the chair. The sounds of the search boomed through the radio's speaker loud and clear.

As more and more details of the search came through, I realized that it was close. Darned close. So close, that some of the voices on the radio were coming from the southeast side of Pillsbury Mountain. That was my turf!

"Subject is 37 years old, with medium length light brown hair, a mustache, and a beard. His given first name is Edward, but he goes by 'Jerry'."

Jerry! My Jerry? My "I've been in these woods since I was carried in" Jerry? No; it just couldn't be. He surely could've found his way out with blindfolds covering both his eyes. (That last sentence has been coated with a moderate dose of sarcasm.) Then I remembered: yes, he did have on a red woolen shirt, and he was wearing a pair of dark green pants. And he certainly did have a rifle, although my knowledge of firearms (or lack thereof) precluded me from identifying the make and model.

Yup—it sounded like Jerry.

I must admit that, at first, I had to control a bit of chuckling. I knew that it wasn't right to laugh at someone else's expense, especially when they were lost in the woods overnight. But somehow, I just couldn't help it. The chuckling continued even as I called the rangers down below to report my contact with the victim the day before. Assuming that Jerry was OK, he was going to emerge from this incident with a major amount of egg on his face.

As I recall, it didn't take the rangers long to locate their quarry. He had simply wandered off of his intended track, which was to take him back to his truck on the main logging road. Not reaching any place before dark, he had made a small fire and settled down for the night on the southwest side of Pillsbury Mountain. By early afternoon, the search was over, and the red-faced "subject" was given a lift back to his vehicle.

I had a chance to discuss the case later on that month with one of the local Conservation officers who was called in on the search. He had been with the DEC for many years, and had pretty much "seen it all," but even he was amused by the irony involved.

"Yeah, he was a bit of a cracker, that one," he smiled as he recollected the brief operation. "Once we found him, he suddenly seemed to know exactly where he was. He said he had gotten a bit 'turned around,' and had decided to wait until daylight to start walking again."

"Did he act embarrassed about you folks having to go in and find him?" I asked.

"No, not really," the officer responded. Then, looking slightly puzzled, he turned his eyes towards me and said, "Y'know, if I didn't know any better, I'd say that he was even a little bit per-turbed that we went in to find him at all, saying that he could've gotten himself out of there sooner or later. After all, he told us, 'he'd been in those woods since he was carried in!'"

—18—

Lost!

It happens to all of us, whether we want to admit it or not. Sooner or later, unless you're zealously following the trail markers, you will get "turned around" once in a while. It can lead to some rather harrowing moments, especially if you're twenty miles or so from the nearest road.

Whenever I think of being lost, I always remember a line used by the character "BJ" in the television series M*A*S*H. One afternoon, their truck breaks down in the middle of nowhere, with enemy troops lurking nearby. Scanning the hostile countryside around them, he quips, "We're lost. I've been lost before, and this is exactly what it looks like." It's a common feeling that can be quite unnerving. You think you know where you are, but nothing looks familiar.

In an area such as the Adirondacks, there are truly several different "levels" of being lost. Many times, hikers get confused as to where they are on a particular trail, which can cause them to turn onto a different trail, or something equally as harmless. This is not usually a dangerous situation, as they can usually retrace their steps and "find themselves."

An alternative, which is far scarier, is the individual (or group) who attempts to go someplace that is not directly on the trail, and then loses their bearings. Without any references people have been known to wander for days on end without finding their way out. That can lead to an extremely frightful experience, especially if it is a lone hiker.

All the outdoors books in the world give pretty much the same advice for the person who suddenly finds himself lost: stop, sit down, and think for a moment. Take a good look around you, climb a tree if necessary, try and regain your bearings. But whatever you do, don't panic and take off in a high-speed gallop, because it usually just compounds the situation.

However, people are not always guided by logic, especially in instances where survival might be an issue. I found, in my years as a ranger, that the differences in reactions between groups who are "turned around" can be so huge that it can actually be rather comical.

What follows here is just such a contrast: It is the story of two different groups who I encountered during the same summer. Neither one had the slightest clue of where they were, or how they had gotten there. But their reactions and emotions were at the farthest extremes of the spectrum, and the contrast still sticks in my mind some fifteen years later.

The first was a Boy Scout troop that had hiked in from the Moose River Plains, which formed the northern boundary of the West Canada Lakes wilderness area. They actually hiked in via the Otter Brook Trail, which was unusual. Very unusual. The trail comes into Cedar Lakes from due north, and intersects the Northville-Lake Placid Trail about half a mile east of the Cedar Lakes dam. In the entire time that I had been back there, I had never seen the trail used, ever. For some reason, people avoided it like the plague.

It was about 7:00 P.M., and I was staying in the easternmost lean-to on Cedar Lakes. The day had been rather warm, and the heat and humidity had hung around into the evening. There was a group of campers staying at the same lean-to, three young men who were casually hiking from Piseco (to the south) towards Wakely Dam (to the north) over a one week period. They were only covering about five miles per day, then stopping to relax and enjoy the fishing. Ah, yes, my kind of hiking!

We had eaten dinner, and had thrown some extra wet leaves and vegetation on the fire, which was supposed to make enough smoke to keep the blackflies and mosquitoes at bay. I strolled over towards the lake, and was preparing to get some water to take back to the lean-to for "KP" detail.

Suddenly, I heard the sound of heavy feet thundering wildly over the dirt. At first, I thought that the DEC had decided to introduce buffalo to the Adirondacks. I recalled seeing a documentary about bison a few years earlier, and the sound was remarkably similar.

I turned around just in time to see two bodies, both hurtling towards me at high speed. One was an older boy, around fourteen, while the other was a younger fellow, perhaps ten or eleven. They both had panicked looks about them as they flew over the ground.

"Water! Where's the water? We need water!" They hollered in unison. Then, to my surprise, the younger one (who may have been unable to stop in time) tripped over a log by the shore and went flying headfirst into the lake.

With that, one of the campers at the lean-to nonchalantly looked down at the poor lad in the lake and said "I don't know how much water you need, but I assume that this (nodding towards the lake) is enough!"

After pulling the boy up out of the shallows, I was able to quiet them both down long enough to ascertain that they were part of a much larger group, and that some of them might be in trouble. They were lost, and they had run out of water. They had been hiking all day long over the Otter Brook trail in order to reach Cedar Lakes. And while twelve miles (which was the distance of the hike) may not sound like a lot to an experienced hiker, it can be an awful long way for a ten-year-old tenderfoot who has never carried a pack before.

I decided to take an after-dinner hike with these two scouts, who were chosen to seek help because they were the only ones with enough reserve energy to walk any further. Turning up the Otter Brook trail, we came upon the rest of the troop within the first mile of walking. What a scene it was. There were about twenty five of them, most were lying down. Some were lying next to packs that looked about as big they were. An occasional soft moan could be heard from some of the smaller forms.

I was received like a cavalry unit that had appeared on the scene just in time to save the day. The two scout leaders looked to be as bedraggled as their charges, feet aching and mouths open from lack of drinking water. Evidently, they had not brought much in the way of supplies, as they thought that they would be hiking alongside Otter Brook for the entire time.

After hiking for seven or eight hours, they determined that they were lost, otherwise they'd be at Cedar Lakes already. So they plunked themselves down in the middle of the trail, and decided to call that "home" for the night. (Little did they know they could almost see the lake from their campsite.)

All that I had to do to quiet their nerves was to point out exactly where they were on their map. I then congratulated them on being the first Boy Scout troop to ever complete the entire trail in one day. (I had no idea whether this was a true statement or not, but it visibly perked up the entire troop.) Then, I grabbed six or seven of their canteens, and set off for the nearest spring. They were relieved at being "found," and I came off as being something like a cross between Superman and Paul Bunyan.

But it didn't always end that way. Some groups, thankfully, don't panic at all when they discover that something is amiss. And then again, some groups never even realize that something is amiss. Which brings me to "group number two," and one of the strangest sights ever witnessed on a true backcountry trail.

This incident actually didn't happen to me, but to John Wood, my partner on the trails, who was patrolling the territory between Cedar Lakes northward towards Cedar River Flow. For some reason, John had decided to take a diversion that afternoon and head east in order to check out the Sucker Brook lean-to. It added an extra couple of miles onto his day, but John was an extremely diligent individual who took his job very seriously. As such, this type of activity was not out of the ordinary for him.

John had made it to the Sucker Brook lean-to, and found it empty. This was not unusual, as I can't imagine that it was ever occupied more than four or five nights out of the year. Nobody hiking the Northville-Lake Placid Trail wanted to divert that far from their route to stay there. In order to get to the lean-to from the nearest road, one had to leave Route 30 at the Lewey Lake campgrounds and hike in the first several miles over a rough trail that included about thirteen wet crossings of the meandering Sucker Brook. Then, the trail climbed about 1,000' up a very steep grade, crossing the col between Cellar and Lewey Mountains. Finally, making a steep descent, the trail crossed through some beaver-made marshes in which one false footstep on a log would plunge the unwary hiker into five feet of murky swamp water.

As I said, nobody ever went in to the Sucker Brook lean-to.

John was in the process of sitting in the quiet structure, munching on a granola bar, when suddenly he heard some sounds coming from the trail behind him. It sounded like people, young and old, singing.

"Oh, the bear went over the mountain, the bear went over the mountain, the bear went over the mountain, to see what he could see" came the musical notes.

John got up to greet the arriving party, who were in obvious good spirits. He stepped around the corner of the lean-to, looked back, and froze.

It was apparently a family, much the same as you'd see walking down the boardwalk in New Jersey. Literally. The father had on a pair of swimming shorts and a tee shirt, complete with a pair of swimming goggles dangling from his neck. His wife was dressed in a similar manner, with no hint of any gear that could be used for a stay in the woods. But it was one of the five children who had the strangest piece of gear ever viewed that far into the woods, as they pushed along a small "Sting-ray" bicycle that was popular back then.

I'm aware that bicycles have evolved into a form these days that can go literally anywhere, and I wouldn't be surprised to see one climbing a tree, but they just didn't have that type of thing in 1979, and John was dumbfounded.

Introducing himself, John asked the group just where it was that they were headed with such unusual gear.

"Why, we're just takin' a stroll around the lake!" boomed the father. According to John, he seemed quite pleasant.

"What lake?" John asked in bewilderment. There were no lakes around for miles.

"Lewey Lake, of course!" hollered Dad. "We saw this trail going 'round the lake, and figured it'd be a good day for a family hike. So here we are!"

It took John quite a while to explain to the family that they weren't going "'round the lake," and that they had just hiked eight of the toughest miles into one of the most desolated lean-tos in the entire area. And that bicycle, how did that small youngster push it up over the top of that mountain? There were too many questions to even bother asking.

John quickly realized that he could send this group out of the woods via a much easier route by pointing them a few short miles down the Placid Trail. There, they could be picked up by a ranger's truck nearby the Cedar River Flow lean-to. John could use his radio to notify the ranger's station at Wakely Dam that he needed transportation for the misplaced family, and everything would have a happy ending.

As John went ahead and made the appropriate arrangements, he started to notice something else unusual about the group. It was a total lack of concern about their predicament; not a speck of worry that they were that far into the woods, without food, water, or clothing, and were now about to be "rescued" by a DEC vehicle that would bring them back to their campsite at Lewey Lake. They also displayed no visible signs of the rigorous hike that they had already completed.

If ignorance is bliss, this family was in heaven.

John walked with them down the final few miles to meet the truck. I'm still not sure whether he did this because he was heading that direction anyway, or if he harbored doubts about their ability to navigate the few remaining miles of trail without ending up somewhere in Mexico.

The rest of the trip passed without incident, as John shepherded the boisterous crew down the trail towards the appointed rendezvous. They took turns naming songs, which the entire family would sing in various degrees of unsynchronized harmony. It was a most strange and unusual family. But musical.

As they happily piled into the big red pick-up, John waved, and then turned to start the hike back to Cedar Lakes. Over his shoulder, for quite some time, he could hear the seven joyous voices fading in the distance, all shouting out in unison, "That's all that he could see, and all that he could see, was the other side of the mountain...!"

—19—

Bob Learns Respect

Wow! It had to be the brightest tent that I'd ever seen. It wasn't exactly red, and it wasn't exactly orange. It was somewhere in between.

It was a Tuesday afternoon, and I was headed south towards Piseco on the last leg of my weekly patrol. My weekend would start within a matter of a few short miles. A lazy rain shower had followed me throughout the afternoon, dripping off the trees and bringing out the red eft newts that scurry across the trails. The weather was fairly cool, although that's to be expected in early June. All in all, it was one of those days that I had learned to accept on a philosophical level; existing out in the rain was just one more thing that I shared with the creatures that surrounded me on a daily basis as I went about my business.

I was within three miles of the Piseco trailhead, and hadn't counted on seeing anyone else that afternoon. Very few people ever started a hike in the rain; and there were no more popular camping spots in the few remaining miles of trail.

That's when I saw it.

Maybe it was just the overall contrast of the bright plastic material with the gray, overcast skies that emphasized its color. After all, most campers in our area carried tents of fairly "woods-neutral" colors, such as green or gray. This one, however, was not only red; it screamed "RED!" It was visible from a distance of several hundred yards, and that was through some rather dense trees. I have no doubt that, had it been the middle of a dark moonless night, it would have been just as visible.

As I approached, warning signals starting going off in my head. Whoever occupied this tent had "tenderfoot" written all over them.

A closer examination of the tent confirmed that it was a $19.99 discount special, made for pitching in the backyard. Its shiny plastic walls were totally airtight, so as to prevent the circulation of air inside the structure. This usually results in a huge amount of condensation forming within a tent, allowing the hapless resident to wake up drenched in his or her own fluids. It was also constructed of the flimsiest of materials, which are usually not fire resistant. I noted the department store price tag that was still attached and flapping gently in the wind.

On top of everything else, this camper had decided to erect his tent smack dab in the middle of the trail! The current law stated that tents had to be set up at least 150 feet away from all trails, lakes, streams, etc., and I often had to do some minor public "education" on this point. After all, folks very seldom strayed that far from any of these major landmarks, and I tried to be quite lenient when enforcing the regulations. But this was ridiculous! I was half tempted to walk directly down the middle of the trail, blazing a path that bisected this contraption.

Just as my curiosity peaked, I detected a furry head through the window of the tent, and a pair of dark eyes glaring up at me.

"Hey man, what's up?" came a rather groggy voice from inside. "You work back here?" It was alive!

"Sure do," I replied, as I stepped around the front of the tent. "At least that's what people think, although I'd probably do this for free. Where are you heading?"

The young fellow began pulling himself out of his thin cotton sleeping bag while unzipping the tent. "Well, first of all, my name's Bob, and I want to tell you that I've got a lot of respect for you, living all the way back here the way that you do, man. It's really something...I've got a lot of respect for you. I'm heading up to Lake Placid on this trail, and I'd like to ask you some questions, if you've got the time." The whole while he spoke, he continued to wriggle out of his sleeping bag, which apparently had zippers that were as cheaply constructed as the tent. It required some moves that were truly acrobatic, and I marveled at his body control.

I had a good look at Bob as he finally made his escape through the bottom flap of the tent. He had very long, black, wavy hair, and a very long, black, wavy beard. As a matter of fact, there were places where the two of them merged, and I couldn't tell where one stopped and the other started.

We talked for quite a while. Bob was a Long Island resident, which I had guessed from his first "hello." He had never been in the woods before, and had read about this particular area in a recent magazine article.

Bob wanted to know all kinds of things about his surroundings, including some questions I found rather strange. He was very focused on the fishing in the area—to a degree that I'd never heard of before. But then again, some people do like to fish, and make it their primary reason for going back there in the first place. I tried to fill him in as much as possible about the trail ahead of him, as well as where those better known fishing spots might be found.

"Yeah, man, I've never been here before. I've never been any-place like this before. I've got a new respect for the Adirondacks, man," Bob droned on as though in a bit of a fog. At best, he was clearly out of his element. At worst, I suspected that he was lost.

"What do you mean by that, Bob?" I asked.

"Well, I guess I never imagined that New York had anything

like this, y'know?" His eyes were wide as he looked around him, talking slowly all the while. "I guess I never imagined anything nearly as big as this place. I mean, I thought that I'd be able to see through the woods to the nearest city street most of the time, y'know man? But I ain't even seen another camper since I've been back here. And last night, I had a huge bear nosing around the outside of my tent, lookin' for stuff. I'll tell you, man, I've got a new respect for the Adirondacks!"

We talked for about fifteen minutes, during which I learned that Bob was not a run-of-the-mill novice in the woods. Nope, he was in a class by himself!

While talking, I asked him about some of his equipment choices, as I had never seen anyone carry some of the items that he had so thoughtfully packed. One entire side of his pack contained nothing but a five pound bag of flour and a half-gallon of oil. This, was, he explained to me, to cook up all the trout that he'd catch every day along the trail to Placid. Evidently, he was quite confident in his prowess as a fisherman, as he didn't bother to bring along any food, save for a few granola bars.

"Yep," he sighed as he stretched out next to the tent, "this trip I'm just going to live off the land, and see how it treats me. Oh, by the way, how do you like my filleting board? I'd be willing to bet that you haven't seen a nicer one back here in years."

A what? I turned back towards Bob, to see just what he was talking about. There he stood, proudly displaying a huge wooden cutting board that he'd brought from his home kitchen with the sole purpose of gutting his fish. It must've weighed five pounds! And it would be walking all the way to Lake Placid with him. On Bob's back. Oh my, this was getting quite interesting.

I bid Bob farewell, as I was anxious to be moving along, but somehow I knew that I hadn't seen the last of him. And I was right.

My two days off seemed to fly by, as they always did. And when it came time to do the grocery shopping for my next week's patrol, a little voice in the back of my mind kept telling me to purchase a little bit extra, just in case. I stocked up with extra bread, fruit, and pasta.

Friday morning was a very unusual day for June, as the frost was heavy on the ground. I remember completing my packing in a hurry, as I wanted to generate some body heat by starting my hike back into the woods. I was coming in from Perkins Clearing, and would be staying at Cedar Lakes that night. Unless Bob had covered more miles of trail than I expected, I'd run into him sometime during the next day or so, as we were moving in opposite directions. I just hoped that he had at least brought some warm clothes along with him.

Nope.

I arrived at Cedar Lakes a bit late in the day, as I had stopped for a while along the way to clear some small trees from the trail. I set my tent up near the Beaver Pond lean-to, where a nice couple from Quebec were staying overnight. They had evidently passed by the West Canada Lakes lean-tos earlier in the day, and wanted to tell me about a distressed hiker who they'd talked with briefly. They were concerned.

"He was cold, wet, and miserable," was the sad summary that Pierre relayed. "He had two sets of cotton jeans and flannel shirts, both of which were soaked through to the core. He also asked us if he could buy any food from us. We gave him some snacks, but that's about all we could do."

The friendly Canadian looked at me inquisitively, as though looking for approval that they had done all that they could. I know just what he meant; I've often been asked to assist someone by giving them my supplies, just because they hadn't planned ahead. It could sometimes be a mental struggle that pitted your desire to help others against your need to conserve enough supplies for your own safety. You had to draw the line somewhere.

Anyway, I went to bed early that night, thinking that I'd get up before sunrise and start the six-mile hike to West Lake in time to render any assistance that was needed. The night air was very cold and crisp, which is my favorite weather for sleeping. After chatting over the campfire with Pierre and Janet for a while, I climbed into my tent, pulled the sleeping bag over my face, and immediately fell asleep.

It seemed like no time at all before I was awakened, not by the alarm on my wristwatch, but by a rather strange sensation. It felt like someone was lying on top of me. As I woke up, I pulled the sleeping bag away from my head, and found a very cold, crunchy material pressing against my face.

Snow. It was a June morning, and two inches of very wet snow had fallen on top of my tent, collapsing it under the weight. I had not dug the tent stakes in very deeply, as I had not expected this type of thing in June. As I climbed out of tent and started re-erecting it, I heard Pierre's voice call from the lean-to.

"Again? It collapsed about an hour ago, and I set it up while you were asleep!"

Looking down, I noticed that he had indeed placed rocks over those stakes that he'd pushed back in. I must've been in a profoundly deep sleep!

It was about 4:30 A.M., and I decided that it was too late to go back to sleep. Besides, I was getting more and more worried about our visitor from Long Island. If he was cold and wet yesterday, how would he be today, sitting out there in the snow? I knew that I wanted to get going as quickly as possible.

It's always amazed me just how fast one can move along a trail when there's a sense of urgency involved. All the ingredients were there for creating one fantastic case of hypothermia: cold air, moisture, and a poorly equipped novice hiker who probably hadn't eaten in days. I knew that John Remias was out of the woods for the week, so the cabin at West Lake would be locked up, unable to provide assistance. My concerns built as I walked, and I could feel the trail flying by under my feet.

It took me less than two hours to reach West Lake. Upon my arrival, I set out to find Bob, who would probably be in one of the two lean-tos. I guessed that he'd be in the northern one, so I headed off in that direction.

Bingo. I knew that he was there, as I saw the flaming red tent from about two-hundred yards away. As I approached, I noticed that something just wasn't right. It was his tent alright, but it wasn't set up. Instead, it was rolled into a ball in a corner of the lean-to, and there was no sign of Bob anywhere.

The lean-to was a mess. There were unused empty pots and pans strewn everywhere, and cigarette butts thrown far and wide about the floorboards of the structure. His thin sleeping bag appeared to be pushed into the middle of the tent, along with some other articles of clothing. The whole stack was then rolled up into a huge swirling pile, which resembled (in no small way) a four-foot-tall jellyroll. It was interesting. And, I thought, rather artistic. But a mess.

I was in the process of scratching my head and mumbling to myself about Bob's whereabouts when suddenly, the entire heap of stuff started to move. A hairy head poked its nose out of one end, a bit like a snapping turtle looking out of its shell.

Aha! It really was alive!

"Hhhhey, mmmman, it's yyyyou agggain," his teeth chattering. "Hhhhow ya ddddoin'?"

In an attempt to stay warm, Bob had taken every shred of clothing that he had at his disposal and pulled it around himself. It was a sorry sight. He looked like a one-man garage sale. Even inside the thick nest that he'd built for himself, I could see that he was visibly shaking. I knew that he was feeling miserable, but I was even more worried about the possible risk of hypothermia.

Actually, what I wanted to do was to get him warmed up, then get him out of the woods so I wouldn't have to worry about him anymore. But I knew that that might be impossible, after all, I wasn't allowed to kick someone out of the woods for being stupid. No, I'd have to settle for getting him warmed up and fed.

Bob talked the entire time that I got a fire going. He wanted me to know (on a continuous basis) that he had a "new respect for the Adirondacks."

"Hey, man, back home it's probably around seventy degrees out. Nobody will believe me when I tell them that it snowed up here in June."

"Well, this is a little bit unusual," I warned him, "but you've really got to be prepared up here for any kind of weather on any given day. It can get quite cold at night even during the middle of summer, and you're not dressed for it at all. You've got to learn to stay away from cotton garments and use wool and polyesters instead, since they dry so much faster."

We spent the next two hours drying his clothes over the fire. He had been unable to start one the night before. Evidently, he had spent almost an hour holding lit matches underneath a rather soggy, rotten birch log that wouldn't have burned if it had been doused with gasoline.

While we stood next to the warmth of the flames, Bob talked about his friends back home on Long Island. "Yeah, man, I think what I'm going to do is to go back home and read some more about what to wear and what to pack. Then, I'm going to come back up here and bring a bunch of my friends. I mean, I've got a whole new respect for the Adirondacks, man."

I cringed. I had a vivid mental image of six or eight Bob clones running around the woods, making life miserable for all of us. It was more than I could take, and I quickly pushed the thought from my mind.

After feeding Bob the last of my canned fruit, I was able to obtain a sworn promise from the rejuvenated hiker that he'd con- sider leaving the woods as soon as possible for his own safety, via the quickest available route. It helped to have a few hypother- mia stories with unhappy endings tucked away in my memory. They convinced Bob that he was not in the best possible location for his level of preparedness.

The only problem was that he didn't have a car with him. He'd hitchhiked up here from the Island, and had no way to get back to a major city. What to do? I was in a bit of a quandary on this one, and I had no solution. I was still pondering the situation when I heard a noise from behind me.

I turned around, and almost jumped out of my boots. I could hardly believe my luck. It was Joe, my steelworker friend from Utica who was up for his monthly trip through the area. What timing! I felt as though he'd been delivered by a magic genie.

With some misgivings, I asked Joe whether he'd be willing to see Bob out of the woods and give him a lift to Utica on the following day. I knew that I was imposing on Joe's good nature, but I was desperate. I also knew that it would be an interesting walk for the two of them. Joe motored along at a rapid rate, and could easily cover fifteen to twenty miles of trail without thinking about it. Bob, on the other hand, had needed four days to hike fourteen miles. Yup, the possibilities were endless!

I was greatly relieved when Joe said that he'd gladly help Bob out of the woods, though I realized what Bob would be in for when I heard him ask Joe about the ensuing hike, which they'd start early the following morning.

"About how far is it to this 'Moose River Plains' place where you've got your car, man?" asked Bob. "My feet are kind of sore because all my socks got wet and gave me some nasty blisters."

I was about to answer for Joe by telling him that it was about twelve miles to the spot where Joe always parked, when Joe himself chirped in. "Oh, it's not more than about four or five miles at the most. It's really quite short. Trust me!"

I managed to conceal a smile, as I made my preparations to leave for the rest of my daily patrol. Bob was in for an interesting hike that Sunday, and I sort of wished that I'd been there to hear some of their conversation en route to the distant trailhead. I could only imagine that it would be lively.

It was almost a month before I ran into Joe again. This time, he was sitting down on the dam at Cedar Lake, casually dangling a fishing line into the waters below. He looked at me with the expression of a man who's owed a favor. I knew that I did.

"What a trip!" Joe exclaimed without a preamble. "You wouldn't believe what I had to go through to get that guy out of the woods! He started complaining before we even got to Brooktrout Lake," which was only about three miles away. "By the time we hit the half-way point, I thought he was going to drop. I had to keep on telling him that my car was 'just over that next hill', or he wouldn't have made it."

I got a chuckle out of that one, thinking about Joe pushing Bob over the tops of countless "very last hills."

"And then, just when we made it back to the car and I thought we were home free, I realized that he smelled so bad that I'd have to leave the windows open the entire way back to Utica. I froze my tail off!"

"But, I did get something out of the deal" he said, glancing down at his fishing line.

"Oh really?" I asked in surprise. "He didn't seem like the kind of person who'd carry much cash around with him."

"Oh, no, he didn't offer me money for the ride, and I probably I wouldn't have taken it anyway. But he did insist on giving me this huge cutting board. It was pretty nice. I took it home and made a coffee table out of it!"

I laughed. "You must have impressed him quite a bit, Joe."

Joe shot me a sideways glance, "Don't start with me, mister. Anyway, I think he was most impressed with you. He kept talking about how you live back here all season long. I think he wants to come back and visit!"

"Oh no", I groaned. "He couldn't possibly still want to come back here, after everything he's gone through this week."

"Oh yes he does," answered Joe, getting in the last laugh. "He's really looking forward to it. The whole trip home, he kept telling me that he's got a new respect for the Adirondacks!"

—20—

Bible Schoolers and Backwoods Boozers

If my first two years in the woods taught me anything, it was that there are all kinds of people traveling through our area. Most of them were good, considerate individuals who came and went without leaving a trace behind them, except for a name in a registration booth. A few, however, had to be watched over in order to ensure that they would comply with the local regulations.

When meeting a group in the woods, I usually tried to make a quick summary as to their potential for causing mischief. To that end, I was fortunate to be in the West Canada Lakes region, as we often had so few visitors that I could devote a fair amount of time and energy to any one group of potential evil-doers.

One July weekend during my third year on the job, I hiked up the Placid Trail from Piseco, having stayed at Spruce Lake the night before. The trip had been dreadfully quiet, and I had not encountered a single hiker.

I was ahead of schedule, so after leaving Spruce Lake I decided to detour further north in order to check out the lean-to on

West Canada Creek. It was not far out of my way, and I always enjoyed the view from that particular spot.

The lean-to at West Canada Creek sits on the north side of the bridge that spans the outlet to Mud Lake. The lean-to itself is directly on the trail, offering little or no privacy from passers-by. As I descended the trail leading to the heavy wooden bridge, I could see that the shelter was occupied.

Wow! People! I was beginning to think that there was no one around but me. After all, it was a Saturday, and even the West Canadas got visitors on weekends.

As I approached the campsite, I began to get the feeling that something just wasn't "right." The inhabitants were a group of four rather shabby teenagers dressed in heavy metal rock and roll T-shirts and dungarees. They eyed my uniform suspiciously, as though I was a state trooper on patrol. It was a look that I had never received from anyone back there, and I was more than a bit surprised. They did not say a word, not one.

Even as I raised my hand in greeting, the silence continued. It really was kind of eerie. It must have been what school teachers experience when they walk into a bathroom where a group of students have been smoking, but then toss down their butts to avoid getting caught. Everything just stopped, and we looked at each other.

"Hey, how y'all doing today," I sang out, trying to break the ice. "You sure did get yourselves a nice spot for the weekend! Is there anything I can tell you about or give you directions to?" I asked.

A mumbled chorus of "no thank you" was all that I got, along with some rather furtive glances. It was clear that this group did not want me around.

Rather than leave immediately, I decided to spend a few minutes addressing them in a friendly manner. I asked them a few simple questions about their hometowns, and whether they'd ever been back into our neck of the woods before. I was supposed to gather this type of data anyway, and most people really didn't mind the questions.

While we spoke, I glanced around the lean-to, noting the contents of some of the packs. One of them, to my dismay, contained what looked to be a full bottle of whiskey. Oh hell.

I tried to talk with them about their travels, but it was fruitless. They obviously wanted to continue with whatever it was that they were doing, which did not include having someone in uniform present. And so, after wishing them a nice stay, I decided to take my leave.

As I mentioned earlier, my regular route involved heading east, away from the central part of my territory. However, on this occasion, I decided to alter my weekly patrol, in order to keep a closer watch on this group. I had them pegged as "rowdies," and wanted them to know that I was around. I called the Pillsbury Mountain fire tower, and relayed a message out to my boss that I had a potential problem.

"You need any help?" Tom Eakin responded. It was comforting to know that assistance was always there if needed; especially since I had no real law enforcement powers of my own.

"No, that's OK," I answered. "I just want to be able to stay nearby to keep an eye on these guys. I think I'll head down to South Lake and stay in the lean-to there for a night or two."

Tom agreed with me, so I headed off down the trail towards South Lake. It was a little over a half-mile north of the West Canada Creek lean-to, and I'd be able to maintain a vigilant watch from there.

I certainly never minded staying at the South Lake lean-to. In my mind, it was the premier campsite in the entire region, with a white sand beach right in front of the fireplace that allowed you to walk several hundred feet out into the lake. It reminded me of a heated swimming pool in the middle of the woods, and I often wished that my assigned route included staying at that spot.

However, as I approached the lean-to, I became aware of the fact that it, too, was occupied. It appeared to be filled with a group of about twelve boys, ranging in age from ten to fifteen or sixteen. They were accompanied by two older men who were helping them set up camp.

The outward appearance of this group could not have been more different than the last party I'd encountered: the contrast was startling. Every member of this group was well groomed, with short hair and clean clothes. They all seemed to have smiles on their faces and a sense of purpose about their movement. I detected none of the suspiciousness or hostility that I felt from the previous group.

The two older men introduced themselves as the leaders of the Outing Club of their Bible School Boy's Program. They were from the Syracuse, NY area, and said that they made annual trips through the area, although I had never run into them before. Their cheerful greetings and smiling faces were a welcome sight, so I gladly accepted when they offered me a spot in the lean-to for the night. (It was always easier than setting up my tent, which I very seldom used.)

The rest of the afternoon passed quietly, as I roamed throughout the area talking to the weekend campers. By the time Saturday afternoon rolls around, most folks have normally gotten where they're going and have settled in for the night, so they're usually quite chatty by the time I stop to say hello. As such, I got tied up in several lengthy conversations.

It must have been about 5:00 P.M. by the time I decided to stop back and check on my outlaw friends. After all, I figured, they'd probably have burned down the woods and held up a few convenience stores by then. Maybe they'd even have a hostage or two for me to rescue.

But when I rounded the corner in front of the old lean-to on the Creek, I was mildly surprised. Yes, the same four scruffy rock n' rollers were still sitting there, looking very much like the band of desperados who I'd met earlier. But they were not doing anything out of the ordinary at all. Instead, they were just sitting on the front log of the lean-to, watching a small fire catch onto the kindling that they'd placed below the cooking grate. There were no whiskey bottles out in the open, and there didn't appear to be a hostage anywhere in sight.

Feeling slightly embarrassed, I nodded a greeting, and then continued past their lean-to and across the bridge as though making a quick patrol to the south. However, I doubt that I really fooled them, especially since I had to retrace my steps shortly thereafter in order to return to South Lake.

As I marched back to my lean-to, I did quite a bit of thinking about my original assessment. Perhaps I had been wrong; maybe they didn't need supervision, and I had stuck around needlessly. Oh well, it really didn't matter all that much. And, as I said, I welcomed the opportunity to stay at South Lake for a few days.

The thoughts were still running through my mind as I strolled into the South Lake lean-to. The religious schoolers were all there, and they were raising quite a commotion, as this is bound to happen whenever you get that many enthusiastic young hikers around a campfire. They chattered loudly as they prepared their evening meals, with everyone trying to talk over everyone else.

I opened my food sack, and prepared a simple bowl of noodles, which I usually ate with pieces of bread and vegetables. In an attempt to have some genuine "veggies" that week, I had even carried a few real carrots into the woods, packed carefully in the bottom of my bag. For once, I was not going to eat those dehydrated "just add water and boil" substitutes. I was famished, and I eyed the first carrot hungrily as I raised it to my mouth and took my first bite. This was going to taste great.

It was simultaneous; the first loud CRUNCH of the carrot came in perfect sync with the start of their prayer song. It couldn't have been timed any better if a conductor had given us a cue.

Oh, hell. What to do?

For a short while, I sat there as the group sang their hymns, listening to their harmonized voices over the crackling of the fire. Then, slowly, I tried chewing again. CRUNCH, CRUNCH, CRUNCH!!! It had to be the loudest carrot in the world, and the rest of the ones in my bag looked equally as crispy. Closing my mouth over the large vegetable didn't seem to help reduce the decibel level coming from my molars, which was attracting unapproving stares from some of the youngsters. I decided to take a walk, as the evening was turning out to be quite pleasant. My carrot wouldn't bother anyone if I munched while strolling along the trail.

The following morning, I arose fairly early. The church group was making preparations to break camp early, as they wanted to head south to spend a couple of days at Spruce Lake. I would be heading the same direction within a day or so, but for the time being I wanted to stay within range of the "rowdies" down at West Canada Creek. I was still suspicious.

I took a quick trip up to visit John Remias at the caretaker's cabin, and then toured around the West Lake lean-tos. Most of the folks up there were getting set to hike out of the woods, as it was the end of the weekend. I said farewell to the various groups who were departing, and then headed back towards the South Lake lean-to. After all, I did want to bid farewell to the nice group who I had stayed with over the past two days.

Arriving at South Lake, I found that I was a bit too late to say goodbye, as they were already gone. My pack and sleeping bag sat in the middle of the now vacant lean-to, surrounded by an assortment of empty cans, bags, and other trash. They had simply walked off and left their garbage from the entire weekend sitting there, as though a park custodian would come by at dusk and whisk it away. Angrily, I made a mental note to catch up with them the following day, when I knew they'd be camped at Spruce Lake.

I packed up my belongings quickly and headed down towards West Canada Creek, as I wanted to catch the group of roughnecks before they packed out. After all, if a group of reverent hymn-singing chorus boys left a mess behind them, I could hardly wait to see what was in store from this crowd. I fully expected to find them passed out in their sleeping bags following a long weekend of over-imbibing. I approached their hideout with caution.

For the second time that day, I was too late. They must have left quite early, as the coals in the fireplace had almost completely burned out. I looked around the lean-to, searching for the damage that I felt certain must have been inflicted. But to my surprise, there was none. There was also no garbage, litter, or any trace of the usual things that people leave behind, such as tin foil in the fireplace, etc.

I took a quick walk around the back of the lean-to that had been invaded by the rowdies, and made another interesting discovery. There had been a bit of a garbage pile left there over the years by sloppy hikers who just didn't care enough to clean up after themselves. To my surprise, it was gone. The freshly scraped surface of the ground quietly testified to the fact that my renegade bunch of long-haired hikers had gathered up the old trash pile, and had packed it out.

I had misjudged these people badly, and unfortunately, there was no way to apologize.

The following day, I set out towards Spruce Lake, intent on reprimanding the large congregation from Syracuse. One of the leaders had told me where they'd be camping, which was on top of a nice little rise near the north end of the lake. It was a pleasant location between lean-tos, with a cool clear spring and plenty of firewood handy. As a matter of fact, the only drawback to the spot was that it was dangerous to start a fire there, as there was no fireplace present, and the pine duff* was quite thick.

I arrived at the Spruce Lake campsite by early afternoon, and found the area deserted. They must have decided to stay only one night, and I was stuck "holding the bag" of their trash. Once

*A mixture of organic materials, including leaves, pine needles, small branches, and other decomposing plant parts that will burn if exposed to a flame. Fires should never be started on this type of "soil," as they will burn down into the ground, possibly resurfacing days or even weeks later in the form of a forest fire.

again, I was just a little too late. It was becoming a recurrent theme that week, and I was getting tired of it.

Cursing my luck, I prepared to hit the trail again. Who knew, maybe if this group was moving slowly enough, I could catch up to them. I was about to get going when suddenly, I noticed something coming from the ground. It was a wisp of smoke, and it was coming from the remains of the fire that they had set the night before. Right on top of the pine-duff. They hadn't even bothered to put it out!

Anyone who has ever tried to put out an underground fire, even with the aid of good tools, knows that it can be rather backbreaking work. And I didn't have any tools. Instead, I had my canteen and a two quart cook pot.

The rest of the afternoon was spent running down the fifty foot drop to the lake, filling up the canteen and the pot with water, running up the rise, dousing the fire, and digging with the pot. Every so often, I'd dig my hand underneath the duff in the sunken fire pit, where I'd feel the high heat of the smoldering leafy ground. I had to keep going.

It was early evening before I was sure that the last embers of the fire were extinguished. By then, there was absolutely no chance of ever catching up with the religious school group, so I plunked myself down into a lean-to and called it a day. I had "lost the war," and I didn't feel real good about it.

Later that summer, while reviewing my hand-scrawled notes about the two groups from that weekend, I was able to laugh at my initial summary. It read:

"Encountered group of four potential troublemakers at West Canada Creek lean-to. Am backtracking to South Lake to stay with church group while policing the situation."

Guess I'd been keeping an eye on the wrong group!

Moving Up the Hill

To say that my first year as a Wilderness Park Ranger went by quickly would be the understatement of a lifetime. The weeks and months between April and August blew past with frightening speed, and the end of the season appeared to be right around the corner. As a matter of fact, I was beginning to view the calendar with something akin to panic, as I just didn't want it all to end.

The reason for this was obvious to me; I loved my job. During our initial ranger training sessions, I recall telling another park ranger that I'd have probably taken the job for free. The response I received was that, "The thrill wears off, and after a while, it's all Point A to Point B." Thankfully, that never happened to me, and I loved every minute that I spent in the woods performing my duties.

The park ranger positions in the West Canada Lakes were due to end during the first weeks of September, as usage dropped dramatically after Labor Day. Very few of the other park ranger positions continued beyond that date either, with the exception of the High Peaks, where they stayed busy throughout most of the winter as well. And so, with fall approaching, I was preparing to start searching the area for employment, hopefully just to tide me over until the following April when the next ranger season would start.

It was during the last weeks of August that I got a call from my boss, Tom Eakin, who "wanted to talk to me about a few things." This was a bit unusual, as I very seldom saw Tom. He was an extremely busy man who was tasked to cover a large territory. In general, he had trusted me to do my job with minimal supervision, which I appreciated. So I was more than a little bit curious by the time I reached his house in Lake Pleasant.

"When's your job scheduled to end?" Tom asked abruptly. He never was one for beating around the bushes, and now was no exception.

"Well, I've got another two weeks back in the woods, and then I've got a couple of days to wrap up my paperwork and turn in my equipment," I responded. "I should be gone by the second week in September."

"How'd you like to stay on through the end of November?"

"Yes!" I shouted. "But how...where, I mean...what's up?" I was ecstatic, but I didn't have a clue what was going on. I knew that our jobs weren't funded beyond September, but I also knew that Tom wasn't the joking kind of person. He must've meant what he said, and I wanted to hear more.

"As you know, the tower up on Pillsbury Mountain has been vacant all year long," he explained. "I've got permission to put an observer up there through the end of November. It'll give you two more months of work back there, and the job is yours if you want it."

Did I ever! I agreed on the spot, and we began talking about the duties and responsibilities of running a fire tower.

For anyone who has never visited a fire tower in New York State, they can vary dramatically from one to the next, especially in features such as size and location. Some towers are quite remote, and require lengthy climbs in order to reach the mountaintops on which they're located. Others, however, are extremely accessible, and I've even heard of a fire tower that is situated in the middle of a field.

Pillsbury Mountain was at the extreme end of the first category. In order to reach the tower, one had to drive along a dirt logging road for six miles until reaching Perkins Clearing. The next three miles were also along a dirt road, although that stretch had to be hiked at the time, as public vehicles did not have access beyond the gate at Perkins Clearing. Then, the last two miles were the trail, which crossed the Miami River and proceeded straight up the side of the mountain. It was no small wonder that the Pillsbury Tower received fewer visitors than almost any other fire tower in the state.

I learned rather quickly that the job of forest fire observer would be drastically different from my life on the trails. Tom described the tower on the top of the mountain, as well as the wooden cabin which lay nearby. Most of my time would be spent somewhere between those two structures, as I'd sit perched on top of the 3,600' mountain looking for fires. I didn't know what to expect.

Over the past several months, I had often walked along the dirt road that went past the start of the trail leading up to the top of Pillsbury. The two-mile climb from the bottom to the summit included a vertical ascent of about 1,500'. For some reason, I had never actually climbed the mountain, although I had spent hours looking at it from different locations. There were a few places around Perkins Clearing from which it was possible to see the tower itself; especially when it caught the afternoon sun and reflected it back down the side of the mountain.

The following Thursday, I met Tom back by Perkins Clearing. We were carrying a full load of supplies for the cabin, including food, batteries, and the tower radio, which weighed a considerable amount. Feeling the weight of my pack as I heaved it into Tom's truck, I realized that it would be a slow climb up the side of the mountain.

And slow it was. The two miles of trail seemed like ten, as we trudged up the incline, putting one foot in front of another. I was in extremely good shape at that time, but I was not used to carrying that much weight. It was excessive.

Tom was interesting to walk with, as he knew quite a bit about the animal tracks that appeared frequently along the trail. At one point, he stopped and pointed out a single print, which he identified as the front paw of a bobcat.

"Whenever you see them, they'll always be crossing the trail. They'll never walk along it," he explained. I examined the imprint, and didn't recognize it as anything that I'd ever come across before. But I did spend a minute or so looking at it, just so that I could catch my breath.

About an hour later, the ground finally started to level off beneath our feet. Looking around, I noticed that the trees were now small conifers, with an occasional birch mixed in. The trail was definitely approaching the top.

As we rounded a final curve in the path, the tower and cabin came into view. The tower was a rather ancient looking relic, with wooden stair boards and a shiny silver enclosure that was suspended over sixty feet in the air. But it was the cabin that drew our immediate attention. It was a mess.

Approaching the building, it was obvious that vandals had been at work during the year the tower had lain dormant. The wooden window covers that had been installed to protect the cabin throughout the harsh Adirondack winters had been hacked to pieces, smashing many of the windows that were underneath.

As we unlocked the front door and went inside, we realized that a majority of the windows in the front of the cabin were broken, and for no apparent reason. This had not been done to gain access to the cabin. It had been done for the sole purpose of destroying state property.

We made a quick tour of the grounds, and then went up to the tower itself. Luckily, it was in good shape, and had escaped damage from the vandals. We set up the radio in the tower enclosure, testing it to make sure that we were transmitting to the other stations in the area. We then went back down below to work on the cabin.

The job of replacing broken windows went fairly quickly, as the cabin had an adequate supply of spares. The window covers, however, were damaged beyond repair, and I placed them with the woodpile to be split and used as kindling.

Tom spent several hours up there that day, helping me to make the cabin habitable again. We tested out the wood burning stove, which I'd need in the cold nights to come later that fall. We also tested out the propane tanks, the gas stove, and the lamps, all of which seemed functional. As best as I could tell, I was ready to start the job.

By mid-afternoon, Tom was ready to leave, and I was set to start my abbreviated season as the Pillsbury Mountain Forest Fire Observer. After a final look around, we shook hands, and he started back down the mountain.

For a minute or so, I watched Tom as he disappeared down the trail. I knew that I'd have a lot to do up there, and that I had a lot to learn about the job. But I was still excited about being back in the area around the West Canada Lakes for another few months; even if I was only at the fringe edge of the territory.

I ran up the tower and looked around at the scenery. Unfortunately, the side of "my" mountain obscured almost the entire view of Cedar Lakes, and only a small portion of the Beaver Pond was visible. In the distance, however, I could see West Canada Lake and some of its nearby cousins. They looked so remote and wild through the afternoon haze, and I felt a strong desire to return back there as soon as possible.

But for now, I had a job to do. Turning my mind back towards the immediate task, I took hold of the microphone on the tower radio and pressed the transmit button.

"This is Pillsbury Mountain, station KH 5279, in service at 1500 hours."

I was in business.

—22—

Tower Life

My first few days up on the tower were a steady procession of "discoveries." Just finding my way around was an adventure, as I expanded the horizons of my new world beyond the triangle formed by the tower, the cabin, and the outhouse. The top of the mountain contained a few trails which encircled the summit, and lead to some of the places that the past observers had used to conduct their day-to-day chores.

The freshwater spring, from which I'd draw my drinking water, was not located very close to the cabin. Instead, it was situated several hundred yards down the trail, and I do mean down the trail. Because of this, I tried to carry as much water up per trip as possible.

I learned that one of my predecessors had been an elderly man by the name of Smith Howland, although everyone called him Smitty. He was a resident of Speculator, and he had given up the tower job when he was no longer able to make the arduous climb up and down the mountain.

Smitty had done some really nice work on top of Pillsbury, and the ingenious inventions that I uncovered bore witness to his creative mind and handiness with tools. Some of them, actually, were quite simple. For example, he hooked the gutters up to a drain pipe which ran down into a fifty gallon drum. Whenever it rained, the drum quickly filled with water, which he used for cleaning and washing dishes. Because of this, I seldom had to make trips down to the spring more than once a week.

Some of Smitty's other creations were even more inventive. Among the furniture on the front porch was a wonderful three-legged chair, which he had fashioned out of birch branches and plywood. I never could figure out just what it was that held it together, as I never could see any signs of nails or screws. But it was quite sturdy, and extremely comfortable as well.

In the front room, he had built a small oven, which I found sitting atop the sheet-metal wood stove. It had a couple of wire racks inside, and a temperature gauge on the outside of the door. It worked by placing it directly on top of the wood stove, which provided the heat. The next week, I tried carrying up a package of banana bread mix, which I found quite easy to prepare in the makeshift baker. I was impressed.

Further tours around the summit continued to turn up new surprises. Evidently, Smitty had dug out a pit in back of the cabin that filled with ice cold water. Even in the middle of summer, he could keep items such as milk and cheese fresh by immersing them in a container in the water.

In addition to exploring my surroundings, I knew that I had work to do. I had to become knowledgeable about the "ins and outs" of being a forest fire observer. This would include becoming intimately familiar with the territory surrounding the fire tower. This was no small task. The old time observers who had spent a number of years sitting in one tower could spot a smoke from many miles off just by the change in hues in the country-side. It was a talent that was not developed overnight.

But not to worry, I was ready. What I lacked in experience, I would make up for with my sharp young eyes. So, bright and early on my first full day on duty, I climbed the tower stairs and plugged in my radio. "Signing in" at 8:00 A.M. with the rest of the towers, I sat down on the stool and studied the map that was glued to the table in the middle of the tower.

I was set. I was poised. I was vigilant. Then, I looked out the window. I was blind.

The tower was surrounded by a dense layer of clouds that prevented me from seeing much of anything beyond my own cabin. I felt like I had been suspended by a rope into the middle of an oversized vanilla milk shake!

I sat there for quite a while, trying to figure out just what it was that I was supposed to do. After all, it would be tough to see a fire, unless one started in the cabin. Was I supposed to sit up there and look out the window anyway? It seemed like a bit of a waste of time, but I did it.

I soon learned that, on most mornings, it took an hour or two for the clouds to lift high enough to provide a view from the tower. Before that, the top of the mountain was usually embedded in its own private cloud bank, blocking the view in all directions. When this happened, I'd spend my time working on cabin repairs, or perhaps even sawing and splitting wood for the stove.

Pillsbury did have one modern convenience that I wasn't used to having at my disposal: a working telephone. Well, at least it was a part-time working telephone, as it was a bit shaky at times, especially after it rained. Evidently, the squirrels enjoyed chewing on the insulation, which in turn allowed water into the wiring. As such, I often had a lot of static on the line, making it difficult to hear the person on the other end. At times, though, the reception was quite good, and it was nice to be able to call my family from time to time."

The phone line had been installed, no doubt, to augment the communications system in case of an emergency. However, in the face of extreme boredom, my mind began to dream up a slightly more entertaining use of the ancient handset. I always thought that it would be fun to call one of those pizzerias that advertises "we deliver to your door within twenty minutes or the next pizza's free."

One of the sharpest contrasts between the tower job and my previous life on the trails was the amount of physical exertion (or lack thereof) involved. I learned quite quickly that the job of a forest fire observer was a fairly sedentary existence. As a matter of fact, it didn't take long before some of the forty or so pounds that I had shed on the trails that summer mysteriously started to reappear, making my new 32" waistline pants feel awfully tight. To increase my exercise, I tried taking noontime strolls on the mountain, and added a few basic calisthenics to my day. ("Pillsbury push-ups" became a twice-a-day routine.) But the truth of the matter was that there was very little to do while living on the top of a mountain.

One of the simple, though non-physical, activities that I enjoyed was listening to the conversations that were passed back and forth between the various towers, rangers, and headquarters. Conversations of a personal nature were discouraged during the workday, as the circuit had to be kept open for business use. However, during the evening, some light conversations could be heard, and it reminded me somewhat of truckers using their CBs to stay in touch.

It was very seldom that I could hear any of the wilderness park rangers, as their radios were portable, and had much less power than the larger sets found in the fire towers. Also, they were usually down behind a mountain somewhere, making it impossible to send a signal that I could receive.

Every once in a while, I could hear my ex-partner from the trail, John Wood, as he tried to reach either Wakely or Pillsbury Mountain fire towers. His signal was weak, but usually readable, and I always paid particular attention to the weak signals that I received, in case it was John in need of assistance somewhere.

Once I started working on Pillsbury, I kindled an interest in locating and climbing the other mountains in the region that had fire towers on their summits. This was a lengthy list, as the State of New York used to have 108 active fire towers, many of which were located within the Adirondack Park. While many of them had already been closed down, replaced by aircraft surveillance flights, a good number remained open. These included Wakely, Blue, Gore, Hadley, Kane, Spruce, and Cathead Mountains, some of which are closed today. (A movement is underway to reopen others, with manning provided by area volunteers.)

I probably would never have gotten into the hobby of "tower bagging" if it weren't for a visit that I received during my first week up on the mountain. It was a fairly pleasant sunny day, with decent visibility. I was down in the cabin, making myself a bite to eat, when I heard the radio spouting out my call sign.

"Pillsbury Mountain, this is Kane Mountain, over."

Kane was a smaller mountain located to the south of my area, and I often heard the observer as he talked to his local ranger about area fire conditions. Even without hearing him identify himself as Kane, I would have recognized his voice.

I turned to grab the microphone, but made a rather unnerving discovery, the radio wasn't in the cabin. And I knew that there was no way to hear the radio in the cabin when it was plugged into the tower. It was just too far away. Then, I heard it again.

"Pillsbury Mountain, this is Kane Mountain. Are you there, or are you taking a nap?"

What! What was going on? I dashed across the room to look up at the tower. That's when I saw the two young men climbing up the front stairs of my cabin, both with rather wide grins on their faces. I had been duped!

Coming inside, the fellow in front extended a handshake and introduced himself. "Hello, Pillsbury Mountain! I'm Rick Miller, from Kane, and this is my friend Mike. Sorry about the practical joke, I hope you didn't mind?"

"Hell, not at all," I replied. "You're my first visitors up here.

Welcome to Pillsbury! I'd offer you something to eat and drink, but I don't really have much up here in the way of provisions yet. But have a seat and make yourselves at home."

"Oh, we can help out with that," Rick said, taking his daypack off his shoulders. "We came with lunch for three!" With that, he pulled out a package of frankfurters, rolls, and assorted condiments, which he laid out on the table in the front room. "We kind of figured that you'd have your hands full, with getting the place operational again. Was there much damage to fix up?"

I explained to them about the vandalism that we'd had to repair, and about all the windows that had to be replaced just to make the cabin habitable. It seemed like an old story to Rick, who had been stationed on Kane Mountain for several years.

"It hardly makes sense, does it?" he asked sadly. "The people who break in here don't do it for need of food or shelter. They just simply enjoy ruining things. You should see the condition of some of the cabins on the mountains that have been empty for a few years. Many of them don't even have doors left on them. The cabin on top of Snowy (located northeast of Pillsbury, in the town of Indian Lake) has a big hole in the living room floor where somebody started a campfire! People act crazy sometimes; I just can't figure it out."

As I talked with Rick, I discovered that he had accumulated a vast knowledge of the locations and histories of the fire towers in New York State. Although only in his twenties, he had visited a number of these sites. He was also familiar with many of the people who had served on the various towers over the years, and recalled quite a few interesting anecdotes about some of the old-timers in the area. He was as good a source of "tower info" as I had found, and I was enjoying the conversation.

While we were talking, Mike was busy at the gas stove, cooking up the entire batch of hot dogs. Out of the corner of my eye, I caught a glimpse of him using the spatula to actually flip the dogs up in the air, which I had never seen done before. I couldn't see the point of doing this, but they weren't my hot dogs. When I looked back at Rick, he gave me a subtle "don't ask" kind of smile, rolling his eyeballs upward.

OK, I wouldn't ask.

It wasn't long before lunch was ready, and we sat down to what was my second meal of the noon hour. As we ate, I noticed the sharp contrast in appearance between my two visitors. Rick looked every bit the part of the sturdy ranger/observer. He was sharp, knowledgeable, and in good physical condition. Mike, however, looked as though he was in a bit of a fog. His dark brown hair and wavy beard gave him a bit of a wild appearance, and his eyes didn't appear to move at the same time. It was a bit unsettling.

"You like olives?" Mike asked, as he extracted a jar from his pack.

"Why certainly, especially if they're at the bottom of a rather dry martini," I joked.

"Yeah, I kind of like them myself," he mumbled, "especially the juice. I really like the olive juice." And with that, he unscrewed the lid of the jar, tilted back his head, and chugged the entire jar of olives, juice and all!

My mouth was on the floor, although Rick looked at me as though this was nothing out of the ordinary from Mike. He simply shrugged his shoulders and smiled. Mike giggled, let out a belch, and started on another hot dog. It would be that kind of a day.

The rest of the afternoon was spent up in the tower, where Rick showed me many of the tricks of the trade, including how to scan the horizon for smoke, and how to handle "fire flights" from the tower. These fire flights were small aircraft that were contracted by the state to fly predetermined patterns in search of smoke from forest fires. (They ended up replacing the towers in the capacity of forest fire detection.) They checked in with the fire towers at various points throughout their flights, and reported any unusual conditions if sighted. I was relieved that Rick was able to instruct me on this procedure, as I had already tried to coordinate such an effort earlier in the week, and had

made a bit of a mess doing so. But then again, there was no formal training for the job, so I had to learn as I went along. Sometimes it wasn't easy.

Rick and Mike stayed around for most of the afternoon, helping out as much as possible. Rick went down to the cabin, and
located the old bow saw that Smitty had brought up the mountain. Then, he started cutting and splitting the spruce logs that
had been stacked the previous year. I didn't have much in the
way of hardwood on top of Pillsbury, so I burned quite a bit of
spruce and hemlock. By the time late afternoon rolled around,
an impressive pile was split and stacked neatly on the front porch.

I offered to let them spend the night in the cabin, however,
they declined, and started making preparations to leave in order
to be down before dark. Rick invited me over to Kane Mountain,
which I did want to visit. After all, he had been so helpful, and I
wanted to see what some of the other towers looked like.

"Maybe we'll come back next week and help you get some
more wood cut," Rick suggested. We can look over the rest of the
original towers."

"Sounds great," I replied. "I'll pick up some extra food, so you
won't have to bring anything along with you. Just c'mon up!"

I really was looking forward to it. I had made some new
friends, enjoyed some good company, and had learned quite a bit
about my job in the process.

As I looked around at the piles of newly split wood, I also
realized that these "neighborly visits" could be quite profitable,
as well. It would certainly be worth the expense of providing
lunch in order to have them visit again. I'd even remember to put
a jar of olives on my shopping list.

Larry's Mountaintop Diner

I tend to do things in a repetitive manner; it is usually due to force of habit rather than some strange compulsion. Not that I don't think people can have streaks of bad luck once in a while. It's just that it hasn't happened to me personally, at least not while I was enjoying that first summer of peaceful bliss in the depths of the Adirondack backcountry. For the most part, I had gotten the Pillsbury Mountain observer's cabin back to livable condition, and everything was cruising along just fine.

Then came the week from hell.

It came unexpectedly and without warning. No rabbit's foot would have been large enough to fend off this one. If I believed in the power of crystal balls, and had been able to view the coming attractions, I would've stayed home.

The week actually began with a huge amount of promise. Patty had arranged to take the entire week off from work, and would be staying on top of Pillsbury with me. It was the first part of September, but the leaves had started to turn early that year. What could be better than a week in the woods in a cozy cabin, off by ourselves during the start of the fall foliage season?

I had entertained myself the week before by thinking up special meals that I'd prepare and nice walks that we'd be able to take through the brightly colored leaves. Patty had never been back to see this wonderful territory, and this would be just the way to introduce her to it.

I usually spent my days off in Glens Falls, where Patty was working at the time. As always, we had a great time during my Wednesday-Thursday "weekend," but all the while I was truly looking forward to Thursday afternoon, when we'd leave for the mountain. My plan was to leave Glens Falls at 1:00 P.M., get to the Perkins Clearing trailhead by 2:30 P.M., start the hike by 3:00 P.M., and be on top of Pillsbury by 5:30 P.M.

So much for plans.

I can't remember whether it was one major mishap or just a series of small problematic events, but we didn't finish packing until after 3:00 P.M. Not a good start and I remember feeling quite grumpy. As a matter of fact, I was still feeling rather perturbed as I slung all our gear into the trunk of my rusting jalopy.

Well, maybe not all of our gear. I had left my flashlight back in the apartment, which meant that I had one more trip up the long flights of stairs to the third floor, and they were long flights. (I sometimes thought that the apartment sat at a higher elevation than the fire tower on Pillsbury!) I felt my temper flaring as I slammed the car door, perhaps harder than necessary.

After returning with the flashlight, I grabbed for the key to open the car door. "Ok," I thought to myself, "now where did I put the keys?" I dug deeper into my pockets, but I just couldn't locate them. And I had a big key ring.

Ah yes, there they were! Swinging gently back and forth from the ignition switch on the steering wheel of my tightly locked car!

After a good thirty minutes wrestling with a coat hanger, Patty and I gave up and summoned a local police officer, who quickly opened the vehicle by using a flat, metal device that was made for the purpose. He was a good natured fellow who tried to humor us about our predicament.

"Well, at least you folks wouldn't have to worry about walking away from the car with your keys inside. I really doubt that that you'd find a crook willing to steal this thing. Does it run?"

He was having a bit of fun with me, but I really couldn't complain. After all, I was stuck without him, and I did appreciate the help. It was dinnertime when we finally rolled out of town, and I was getting a bit worried about having to do some of our climb after dusk. I knew the trail fairly well, but Patty had never been there before. We'd have to hustle.

The thought was still on my mind as we rattled into the filling station in Warrensburg thirty minutes later. I didn't have enough gas to take us all the way to Perkins Clearing, as my car's aging engine was only getting about a dozen miles per gallon. We quickly refueled, and I turned the ignition key to start the car. Then I turned it again. And again. There are some times when silence is not golden.

Oh hell, what now?

The mechanic lifted the hood and gave it a quick once-over, something I've never done; for despite not being very superstitious, I believe its bad luck to look under a hood of a car unless you get along well with them on a personal basis. I don't.

"Battery's dead," he sighed laconically. He had a long, sad face, and looked as though he was about ready to receive his last rites. "You want me to drop a new one in for you?"

I hesitated, not wanting to tell him that I just spent the rest of my cash paying for the gas. As I recall, I had about $1.75. A new battery was not in the budget.

"Is there any way you could just give me a jump?" I asked hopefully. "I've got a pretty good battery sitting in my garage at home, and I'll probably just use that one, as long as I can get going here." I was gambling that he wouldn't charge me for the jump, as I couldn't pay for it.

Perhaps he was a good soul, or maybe he just wanted to get

my old bomb out of his parking lot before any of his customers saw it. But, for whatever reason, he hooked us up, and by early evening we were on our way once again.

Leighton seemed surprised to see us pull into his yard so late in the day. It was almost 9:00 P.M., and he was going about his evening chores.

"You headin' up the mountain?" he asked, with more than a bit of puzzlement in his voice. "Why don't you just throw your tent up over there, and hold off 'til the mornin'?"

I must admit, it was a sensible idea. Climbing after dark has never been my idea of a good time, especially since Patty would be moving along at a fairly slow pace. Then again, I doubted that she'd really want to sleep outside in the chilly September air. The temperature was dropping, and a bit of a breeze was picking up.

I made the decision. We'd go ahead that night, but just take our time. Anyway, it didn't look like such a bad night out, and we'd be on top within a few hours. Then, we'd be able to throw some logs into the wood burning stove, and presto, warmth! I became convinced that was the way to go.

We talked with Leighton for a while, which was probably a mistake, as my watch was reading 10:00 P.M. before we started our hike. Normally, it took me about half an hour of flat hiking to get to the Miami River lean-to, another forty minutes of uphill hiking to get to the Pillsbury Trail turn-off, and a final hour of steep climbing to reach the cabin and the observation tower.

Not tonight.

We didn't reach the Miami River lean-to until almost 11:00 P.M., and I was feeling incredibly guilty. Patty was tired, as she had been working a lot of late hours that week. Also, she was not used to carrying a pack, which was starting to pull uncomfortably on her shoulders. We were moving along at a snail's pace as we slowly turned off the logging road to climb the ridge that Leighton had affectionately called "Sonofabitch Hill." We hadn't even reached the base of the mountain yet.

The details of the rest of the climb have faded. I remember a lengthy post-midnight rest break before starting the actual climb, and additional moonlit stops on various rocky ledges along the way. I was concerned about Patty, who was fading in much the same way as my car battery had earlier that evening. How stupid had I been?

Still, we pushed upward, with the breaks increasing in duration. I knew that we were closing in on the top, but at this pace I just couldn't estimate how much longer we'd be. By now, we were creeping along.

The sky was beginning to lighten in the east as we struggled over the last stretch of incline and entered the final hundred-yard stroll through the spruce trees to the cabin. Home at last, and not a moment too soon. We were exhausted, and badly needed food and rest. Through the trees ahead, the roof of the cabin began to take shape.

That's when our problems really began.

Rounding the corner of the front porch, I knew that something was wrong. Very wrong. The entire front window frame had been smashed in as though a car had driven through it. It was obviously not a human break-in. No, this was different. This was something very large, and very strong.

The food and chewed-up cans spread out in front of the cabin told the rest of the story. Bears. Maybe one, maybe more. Maybe still here, maybe gone. I didn't know. This was not part of the plan. But so far, nothing had been part of the plan.

The cabin appeared to be quiet in the dark gray light, and my shouts from across the clearing did not draw a response. Moving Patty back another hundred feet, I approached the cabin, throwing an empty can through the now glassless front window.

Nothing. At least they were gone. They'd been here sometime during the last two days, and had eaten at Larry's Mountaintop Diner without leaving a tip.

No, this trip was not going according to plan.

—24—

The Hex Continues

Slowly pushing open the front door of the cabin, I had my first look around at the destruction. Even in the relative darkness, it was obvious that the place had been completely ransacked. Upon lighting a couple of the interior propane lamps, the extent of the damage became more visible—a major disaster. I could see my restful week with Patty disappearing before my very eyes.

All in all, I counted seven window panes that had been broken. Those shards of glass that had not fallen on the porch were spread throughout the three inside rooms of the cabin. There was bear hair everywhere and on everything. I remember thinking that I'd have to write a song someday called, "I've Got the Bear Hair Everywhere Blues."

All of my canteens had been bitten through, as though the creature thought that I'd hidden something edible inside. This is somewhat understandable in bear logic, since they seem to know that canned goods contain food, which is also why they had gone into the pantry and chomped on every single can in the place, with the exception of a few items that I kept on the very top shelf.

Going through the mess, I discovered the food preferences of this particular bear, or bears. They liked corned beef hash, as well as both white and rye breads. They also appeared to be especially fond of raspberry preserves, for they failed to leave any of that behind. The only other item that I found completely missing was my container of maple syrup, which I had last sighted in a brown plastic jug on the pantry counter. I had purchased it as a special treat to put on top of French toast. To this day, I still wonder if they ate the container too, for I never located it in the woods around the cabin.

We cleaned up enough of the bedroom to grab a quick nap, which ended for me shortly before 8:00 A.M. That was when I had to sign onto the radio and man the fire tower.

I was on duty. Climbing the tower steps, I felt even guiltier, as it left Patty to continue with salvage operations in the cabin below.

There was still quite a bit to do in the cabin. I used my lunch hour to staple a heavy plastic sheet over the open window affording the living room some protection from the wind. We continued to clean up the debris, which included some rather unusual finds. One item of interest was the Tolkien novel, "Silmarillion," which I had just purchased. I had not gotten around to starting it, which was unfortunate, because, for a reason only known to the bear, he had decided to consume the first twenty-five pages of text. (He didn't bother leaving behind a book review.)

By the middle of the next day, we had recovered about as much as possible. The bear hair was gone, any surviving possessions were put back in place, and we even restored some order to the pantry. I had carried up enough food to prepare our meals for the week, although our furry visitor had made off with some of my stored ingredients. But we were getting by, which was enough.

It was turning into quite a strange week! It just couldn't get any worse. Could it? Oh well, at least we were pretty certain that the bear wouldn't return. I'd heard that bears seldom enter a building when they know that people are present.

The afternoon was a pleasant one, and we actually started to enjoy ourselves for the first time since arriving. Patty joined me up in the tower, which made the job a lot nicer. Together, suspended about sixty-five feet up in the air in the steel structure, we sat and watched the countryside. The fall colors were beginning to appear, and a warm sun was starting to drop a bit lower in the sky. It was spectacular. This was why I'd brought her up here. Maybe it wouldn't be such a bad week after all.

It was late in the afternoon when the first radio traffic came in about the accident.

A hiker had taken a fall at a popular spot called T-Lake Falls, and several of the local forest rangers had been called in to help with the rescue. I had never been to that particular spot before, but I heard that it could get quite treacherous. The falls were known for their steep, slippery rocks that had caused numerous accidents in the past. It was not a safe place to venture.

We listened intently, as our position on top of the mountain allowed us to hear every radio transmission for miles around, in all directions. Because of this, we were asked to serve as the central relay station for the operation, passing messages back and forth between the rangers and the other rescue personnel who could not reach each other directly. As was expected, we were asked to remain in service throughout the entire night, which was an absolute necessity in order to maintain communications for the efforts below.

As darkness fell, we moved the radio from the tower back down to the cabin. Our mood was rather somber as we monitored the unfolding events. It was becoming obvious that this was turning into a major effort requiring a lot of medical assistance. It was not sounding good.

We sat on the log stumps that I'd brought inside to use as seats, our ears glued to the radio. The inside of the cabin was dimly lit. The low yellow light cast long shadows across the room, adding an eerie effect.

Then came the radio transmission asking for the coroner. The hiker hadn't made it.

I exhaled, and placed my head in my hands. I remember looking at Patty, who was still sitting next to me. She had tears in her eyes.

What a week. We had been through it all, and now a family had suffered a tragedy. It couldn't get any worse. How could it? I personally felt drained, as though I had nothing else to give, physically or emotionally.

Then I heard the noise on the front porch.

What was that? We were ten miles into the woods, and another two miles up a mountain. Nobody ever came up here at night. I peered through the plastic sheet that replaced our front windows and saw brown. Lots of brown. It was dark out there, but whatever it was that was on our front porch was very large, and very brown. And it was moving towards the front door!

I flew off my seat just about the same time that the front door bumped open. I had neglected to push it completely shut, so the door hadn't latched closed.

I've read many interesting stories about the effect of adrenalin on the human body. I believe that it's called the "fight or flight" reaction that gives people superhuman capabilities for very short periods of time. I can testify to the fact that it works.

I am a fairly large person; however, I'm not certain whether this contributed to my strength at that moment or not. I remember hitting the door with such force that the entire cabin shook. I'm still surprised that the door didn't shatter, although it was extremely sturdy.

I was able to lock the dead bolt in the same motion, which would provide some degree of protection, unless the bear decided to re-enter the cabin by the now open front window. I grabbed my double-bladed ax, as I shot panicked glances at the various windows in the living room. Which one would he pick? All the while I was shouting at Patty to lock herself in the bedroom and crawl up into the attic, where she would be safe.

In an attempt to scare off the bear, I began yelling through the front door at the top of my lungs: "GET OUT OF HERE!" my volume bolstered in no small measure by my fear of the creature. "GO AWAY!" As I was doing this, I decided to look through the pinhole viewing device that was installed in the door. And yes, it was out there, right through the door, very large, and very brown. My grip on the ax tightened.

It was about that time when things got even stranger.

My heart was pounding in my chest as I stood by the door. I was holding my ground, giving Patty a chance to hide, when I heard a reply to my screams: "'Ello? 'Ello?" came the muffled sound from the front porch. Funny, but I've never heard a bear speak English before. This one even had a German accent.

In my altered state of mind, it took me a full ten seconds before I realized that I've never spoken to a bear before. As reality slowly sunk in, I had a calmer look out through the peephole. Whatever it was, it was still large and brown, but well-spoken. I unbolted the door and pulled it open, revealing a single, but large, hiker. He was dressed in a brown jacket and brown pants. On his back, he carried a large brown pack, and in his hands he held a brown camera bag. As a matter of fact, if I had to describe him, I'd just say that he was, well, brown.

The gentleman's name was Manfred, and he had moved from Germany to New York City a number of years ago. His accent was still very noticeable. He was very friendly, and apologized for the scare. In return, I tried to help him with his broken thumb, which had been on the other side of the door when I tackled it. What a mess.

Manfred slept in our living room that night, while we moved back into the bedroom. It was a restless sleep, due in part to the sad events of the day, as well as to the radio, which I was still supposed to be monitoring throughout the night.

The rest of the week continued in the same strange way. One mishap followed another, as if in a marathon nightmare. There was no end in sight.

When Tuesday rolled around, I was ready to leave the woods.

I'd never felt that way before. But for now, I just wanted to get out, hoping that this "jinx" would go away.

We climbed down the mountain and back to my car, which required a jump-start from Leighton as I still hadn't replaced the battery. I drove Patty back to Glens Falls, stopping at the bank to withdraw a few dollars from my terminally ill bank account. Back to civilization. Maybe things would improve!

My friends at the auto garage in Northville quickly and professionally replaced my battery with a new one. They even agreed to let me pay for it the following week, as I had already managed to lose the money that I'd just withdrawn from the bank.

Despite losing the money, my spirits were rising, my car was fixed, and this bizarre week was coming to an end. Life was good, and I was heading back to the woods.

I shifted into reverse to back out of the lot, humming a happy tune, for the sun was shining once again.

CRUNCH. I was thrown back into my seat as the car lurched to an abrupt halt. I looked over my shoulder through the rear-view mirror.

Darn it! Now when did they put that telephone pole there?

—25—

More Tower Life

Living in a remote site without much to do can be a mixed blessing. When I think back to those days and compare them to my current harried existence, I can't see how I'd ever objected to the relative inactivity of life on the mountain. I missed my weekly patrols around the West Canadas, and never really got used to the sedentary lifestyle that prevailed on Pillsbury Mountain.

I did find a number of activities that filled up my spare time, although very few of these were productive in nature. I would have actually enjoyed spending some time fixing up the cabin and completing some of the more skilled repairs on the various facilities on top of the mountain. However, I happen to be among the world's least handy people, and am capable of making only the most rudimentary repairs. Power and hand tools of all varieties shudder whenever I come close to them! As such, I didn't feel guilty about not attempting to make major improvements to the structural integrity of the cabin.

The clearing in front of the cabin was quite large, as Smitty had cut several years worth of firewood from the expanding fringes of his front "yard." He always cut down the hill in one direction, and I'd heard it said that it was no coincidence that he happened to have an open view of Speculator from his front porch. From that position, he could see his home at all times, along with the streets that lined the lake in Speculator. It was a beautiful setting.

The clearing in front of the cabin had another advantage, one which I found to be more useful for my purposes. The whole ground was laced with blueberry plants, which pushed out a modest amount of small sweet berries. I don't know whether they were planted, or if they were native to the mountaintop. Either way, I truly enjoyed them, and sprinkled them liberally over the top of my cereal each morning.

As a matter of fact, I enjoyed this bit of fresh fruit so much that I decided to try boosting the yield from the plants by performing some basic horticultural procedures. I carried a bag of fertilizer up Pillsbury, and set about the task of feeding my new crop. (Not that I had great expectations of success; I am known for being terrible with foliage of all kinds, and was once described by a school buddy as being the only person he'd ever met who could kill an artificial houseplant.)

True to form, my efforts to fertilize the local blueberry plants backfired on me. I never noticed any improvement to the fruit bearing plants themselves, although the weeds that surrounded them appeared to thrive from the treatment. As a result, I produced a magnificent field of dandelions and other assorted nuisances that towered over the blueberries, making them somewhat difficult to locate.

In addition to the edible flora on top of Pillsbury, there was some rather unusual animal life up there as well. I was constantly seeing creatures which I had not spotted at the lower elevations of the Cedar Lakes. However, one of the more reclusive inhabitants of the mountaintop I had yet to meet was the bobcat, although I had seen enough of their signs to know that some lived nearby.

I did finally get to see one of these feline hunters after I had been on top of the mountain for about a month. It was very early in the morning, and I had just stepped out onto my front porch to have a look at the rising sun. A group of three or four snow-shoe hares were running around in circles in front of the cabin. Suddenly, one of them broke away from the circle, instead choosing to bound past the front of my cabin and down the trail towards the bottom of the mountain. When it had gotten about thirty feet beyond the back of the cabin, it turned left and bounded off the trail into the woods.

Suddenly, from the back of the cabin came a very small bob-cat "kitten," which gallumped down the trail, hot in pursuit. Not being an animal expert, I couldn't determine if it was hunting or playing. It was, however, obviously chasing the hare, which probably outweighed him by a considerable margin. The cat reached the same rock in the trail before turning left and diving into the vegetation, intent on finding its prey. I didn't hear any scuffle, so I never learned whether the hare had escaped its pursuer.

The bobcat that I spotted was perhaps the most exotic form of wildlife that I encountered during my entire tenure on top of Pillsbury Mountain. However, I was often bored, and sometimes enjoyed entertaining folks with stories and tales of nonexistent creatures of the woods. And that's when a rather crazy idea first started hatching in my head.

Yeah! If lakes could have monsters, and woods could have abominable snowmen, why couldn't Pillsbury have a creature of its very own? No reason, why, no reason at all! All it would require would be the simplest of materials and a very active imagination.

I began to formulate my plan when the first snow started to accumulate on the ground, which was in the early part of October. I knew that I didn't want to do anything as ridiculous as don a coat, especially since the hunting season was still open, and sportsmen occasionally showed up with weapons in hand.

No, I'd have to settle for leaving behind the most unusual of tracks in the snow, hoping to confuse even the most experienced outdoorsmen.

I started by cutting two slices off of the end of a large spruce log. They were each about twelve inches in diameter, and slightly oval in shape. I cut each of these slices to be about two inches thick, so as to hold my entire weight. They would be the soles of my "animal track shoes."

Next, I cut about a dozen slices off of a small birch branch. These would serve as the toes, so I cut them to be about an inch across. I nailed these onto the front side of the larger soles in a pattern resembling a foot.

The final step was to carry up a couple of leather straps, which I screwed into the sides of the soles in order to hold my feet in place. It was a crude arrangement, but after some time, I assembled it sufficiently to serve my purposes.

Now came the tough part—getting it to work. I took my creation outside during a lunch break, strapping on the makeshift contraptions in much the same way that you'd put on a pair of sandals. They were awkward, but they stayed on my feet. I walked for about twenty or thirty feet, almost falling over several times in the process. Then, I turned around to observe the tracks that I'd left behind.

It was hysterical. I couldn't have asked for any better results. The prints were HUGE! They looked as though an elephant had made its way to the top of the mountain for a quick afternoon tour. I considered writing the name 'Hannibal' into the register book!

I didn't have a chance to test out my new invention until that next weekend, when I knew that a few hikers and hunters would usually set out to climb up to my humble abode. I walked through the snowy woods, staying off of the trail until I had reached a point about a hundred feet before my cabin. Then, I slipped on the monster feet, walked onto the trail, and marched the remaining distance back to the cabin. Just for effect, I then left the trail and changed back into my regular boots on a patch of bare rock, so as to leave no clue to my identity. I wanted it to appear as though the monster had simply vanished into the snow; returning to the mythical land from which it came.

I remember laughing the entire way back into the cabin, thinking of the expression on the face of the first person to view the tracks of the "Pillsbury Giant." I just hoped that nobody would take offense to being "had."

As it turned out, I didn't have long to wait. It was still well before noon when I heard voices in the distance as whoever it was came up onto the final shoulder of Pillsbury. It sounded like the youthful exuberance of a child, yelling back to Dad, who was lagging a short distance behind.

When the visitors came into view, I could see that they were probably a father-son duo. The youngster looked to be about ten, and was bounding up the trail with an abundance of energy. His father appeared to be in his early thirties, and had the look of an outdoorsman. He was dressed in wool pants and wool shirt, with a small daypack harnessed on his back. His weathered face looked as though he had spent a lot of time outdoors, perhaps as part of his job.

I was impressed that the boy spotted the tracks first, although his father probably had not gotten up to them yet. The reaction was everything that I had hoped for, and I listened intently through the open window of my living room.

"Wow! Dad, come look at this!" the boy shouted. "What kind of animal did this?"

His father strode ahead to where his son was crouched, pointing excitedly to the giant imprints. However, unlike his son, he did not appear to be overly excited, only a bit curious. He removed a briar pipe from an outer pocket of his jacket, which he then lit with a brass cigarette lighter. All the while, he silently examined the tracks, walking very slowly up the trail towards the cabin.

"Well, what is it Dad, what is it?" his son continued. He looked about ready to jump right out of his shoes. "Is it a moose, Dad? Or a giant bear? What it is, Dad?"

By now, they were close enough for me to view their expressions, and I watched as a calm (and slightly amused) father turned towards the boy to offer his explanation of the event.

"No, Son, it's not a moose, and it's not a bear," he explained patiently. It's a much rarer type of animal, and it's found only in locations where there are bored fire tower observers. Its Latin name is *practicus jokus*!

—26—

Pillsbury Calls In a Fire

I had been on top of Pillsbury for about three months now, and the season was drawing to a close. I had enjoyed my time as a Forest Fire Observer, especially since it had allowed me to spend an extra few months living in the woods. Soon, the snows of winter would render further observation pointless.

Perhaps the only thing that bothered me just a little bit was that I never actually called in a real fire. There was one occasion when I reported a smoke to Tom Eakin, who, it turned out, had already warned me that I'd be seeing smoke from that particular farm. He'd issued a burning permit the week before, and I had lost the notification. So much for my administrative capabilities.

As I watched the horizon week after week looking for the elusive forest fire, I began to feel just a bit like the Maytag repairman. And not without cause; the Adirondacks have earned the nickname "the Asbestos Forest," as they do not catch on fire easily. But when they do, they have been known to be extremely difficult to extinguish. As such, I took my job quite seriously.

I was sitting in my cabin pondering these points one cold, rainy Saturday morning. The entire mountain was completely socked in by clouds and fog, which rolled up the slopes of Pillsbury in a thick, continuous blanket. Visibility was limited to about a tenth of a mile. In other words, it was a good morning for reading.

I had spent the early hours packing up my personal belongings, as I would be leaving the mountain for good on the following Tuesday. My final three days would involve a lot of cleaning, storing, and winterizing inside the small shelter. It was a sentimental time for me, as I knew that I would not be returning to the mountain the following year. Instead, my plans were to head back into the woods of the West Canada Lakes, which I had grown to love over the past summer.

Many worries and concerns preoccupied me as I went about my chores that morning. I wondered whether Pillsbury would ever have an observer again, or if this was the "end of the road" for the old tower. Budget cutbacks had already closed over half of the fire towers in the area, and more were slated to be shut down the following year. Would Pillsbury become another abandoned artifact, left to fall apart over time? I also wondered if my winterizing precautions were serving any useful purpose; after all, if more vandals returned to visit after my departure, they'd surely smash their way into the cabin once again. Maybe it would be wiser for me to leave the front door open?

On top of everything else, I had a growing concern for the final hike out of the woods. As I cleaned the cabin and stacked my belongings in a pile, I realize that the collection of "small, light items" that I'd carried up over the past few months was turning into a mountain of its own. And I hadn't even started adding in the tower radio, cooking pots, etc., which I'd have to pack out as well. How could I possibly carry it all down the hill in one trip?

I decided not to worry about it, as I could always make a second trip back up the mountain, if necessary. (Although I did want to avoid the extra ten-mile round trip if it was at all possible.)

Instead, I made up my mind to relax and put my feet up for a while. After all, it was Sunday, right?

I made myself a cup of hot chocolate, and sat down at the table in the front room with a copy of Yankee magazine. It was a cozy scene; the wood burning stove was in full glory, sending waves of warm air across the pine interior of the cabin. Just outside the window, the frost and light snow of the previous night covered the ground, making it look very wintry across the summit of the mountain. The snow also coated the evergreen bushes which snuggled up next to the panes of glass by my head. I was glad to be inside.

I sank down into my chair, sipping at some cocoa while reading through the advertisements. It was wonderfully quiet, and I was enjoying the peaceful bliss. Time seemed to come to a complete standstill, without meaning or purpose. I could tell that the observers on the other mountains were probably doing about the same thing as me, as there wasn't a peep out of the radio for hours. And after all, what else could they be doing? Given the weather conditions, there wasn't the slightest chance of seeing a thing. (And, given those same weather conditions, you'd need a gasoline truck and a flame thrower in order to get a fire started in the first place.)

As I tried to read the magazine, I began to doze. At least I thought I was dozing, as I started drifting off into a peaceful haze which softly enclosed my body. Maybe I was sleepier than I had thought.

"No!," I said out loud to myself. "You've got too much work to finish up to take a midday nap. Get up and get back to work!" (I'm very good at arguing with myself, as I'm usually one of the only people who will listen to me!) I sat upright and rubbed my eyes, trying to bring my body back to life.

It wasn't working, I was still tired, and my mind still felt like it was surrounded by a haze, which prevented me from even reading the magazine article in front of me. That's when I looked up from the table and glanced around the room, making a shocking discovery. No wonder I felt "hazy"; it wasn't just in front of my eyes. The entire room was cloaked in a haze, and it was getting thicker by the minute.

Uh oh!

I jumped up out of my seat, not sure of just what to do. I hadn't been cooking anything, yet something was definitely on fire. I didn't know what it was, or just how long it had been burning. Unfortunately, I have never had a particularly keen sense of smell, which might have provided me with an earlier warning.

Looking around the cabin, I found the source of the smoke within a few seconds. It was not good news. At the base of the chimney which carries out the exhaust from the wood burning stove, a metal door (which was used to clean out residue from the chimney) had gotten so hot that it had actually started to char the pine wood paneling. I removed the piece of wood that covered the small door, noting that it was completely black and scorched on the inside surface. How far up the inside of the paneling had the fire traveled? Could I get at it with an extinguishing agent? Would my removing the panel allow extra oxygen to get in, further fueling the fire?

It took me a moment or two to settle down and decide on a logical course of action. I opened the front door and a window in order to clear some of the smoke from the room. I figured that if the whole place "went up" quickly, that I'd be able to get out in a hurry. Next, I tried cooling the outside of the paneling with some wet rags. Much to my relief, none of the other paneling seemed ready to catch, although it too was darkened from the heat. The smoke started to ventilate from the room, however the cleaning door appeared to be getting even hotter, and a high-pitched hissing noise sounded ominously like a boiler that was ready to blow up. What was going on?

Unfortunately, the lack of hardwood on the summit of Pillsbury had forced past observers to feed a continuous diet of spruce and other conifers into the wood-burning stove. I had been no exception; I had burned whatever was close by at the time. I doubt that anyone had cleaned out the chimney in years, which would have lead to a dreadful build-up of tar. And now, perhaps, I would end up paying for the neglect by witnessing a bona fide chimney fire. I felt paralyzed by my helplessness.

As smoke continued to filter out of the paneling, I decided that I had to "fess up" and let Tom Eakin know that I was having troubles. After all, the possibility existed that I'd need assistance, and I wanted to call while I still had time. Since the phone line wasn't working, I'd have to use the radio, which would be heard by the entire rest of the world. (Or so I felt at the time.) It was not a call that I was looking forward to making. I mean, how many forest fire observers actually have to call in that their own cabin is on fire. It's pretty darn embarrassing, when you stop to think about it.

Things didn't get any better when I discovered that I couldn't reach anyone on the radio. It was a Sunday, and many people "down below" weren't working that day. Tom was probably in the woods, away from his truck-based radio. And the office in Northville was apparently closed as well, as my calls to their radio went unanswered.

After stopping to ventilate the room again, I went out with an "all points" request for help.

"Any station this net, any station this net, this is Pillsbury Mountain, over."

The response was almost instantaneous. "Pillsbury Mountain, this is Gore Mountain, over." The observer on Gore was an old-timer who shared the same first name as me. We had met earlier that fall, when I'd climbed up the popular ski mountain that held his tower. He was always friendly and helpful, and it felt especially good that morning to hear his voice.

I'm certain that Larry was anticipating a request for weather information, or some other such small talk, as the lunch hour had already commenced. However, I noticed his voice express concern when I described my situation. While I know that it was just my imagination, I could almost feel the other observers on the other fire towers snapping to attention as they listened to our conversation.

"You'd know if it's a real chimney fire," Larry explained over the radio. "The whole house would sound like there was a train going through it, and you'd see flames coming out the top of the chimney. Have you looked at the chimney from the outside yet?"

"No," I responded, "but I was just about set to take some water up on the roof to dribble down the chimney. I'd like to cool it off some."

"I wouldn't recommend doing that, as you'll probably end up cracking the bricks on the inside. Just go outside and tell me what you see coming out of the chimney. And no matter what else you do, LOOK OUT FOR YOURSELF. Remember to leave yourself a route out of the house, and don't try to save any equipment if everything goes up in flames. The state can always buy a new set of radio batteries, but they can't get to you very quickly if you're hurt. Just watch out for yourself!"

I knew that Larry's words of advice were good ones, and I kept them in mind as I stepped outside to check the chimney. No flames. Well, at least that was some good news.

Returning to the inside of the cabin, I used a pair of thick asbestos gloves to disconnect the stove, which I carried outside to the rocks on the front "yard" of the cabin. (It was constructed of thin sheet metal, and didn't weigh a lot.) Then, I used more cool water to further reduce the temperature of the paneling. It had stopped smoking and was cool enough to touch barehanded.

As conditions appeared to return to normal, I was able to relax just a bit. It was sometime in the early afternoon when I realized that the cabin would survive. Throughout the ordeal, it was comforting to hear the continuous flow of helpful hints and suggestions that were coming in by now from the other towers.

The other observers were apparently absorbed in the events on Pillsbury as they unfolded, and remained glued to their radios for those few hours.

My last few days on top of the mountain were spent in the cold. I was afraid to restart the stove, as I did not want a repeat performance of the previous weekend. Instead, I'd let whoever took over the following year bring up some chimney cleaning gear, which probably should have been done years earlier. I felt that I had done my job in saving the cabin. To this day, I'm still grateful that the fire started in the morning, instead of at night when I was asleep in the back room. If that had happened, I never would've known about it until it developed into a full blaze. If that had been the case, there would've been no way out.

The following Tuesday afternoon, burdened with an over-loaded pack that weighed in at about ninety pounds, I locked the front door of the cabin on Pillsbury Mountain and walked away for the last time. Hiking down the mountain with that big load was difficult, as my legs were not used to "putting the brakes" onto that much weight. However, my strides were purposeful, as I knew that I had at long last fulfilled my job as a fire tower observer. Pillsbury Mountain had finally called in a fire.

—27—

More Times with John

The rain was starting to come down more steadily, and the noise from the roof got a little bit louder. John lowered his head and looked out the front window overlooking West Lake, surveying the scene.

"Looks like it'll be coming down for a while. The clouds are darker at the west end. Maybe we'll get something out of the garden after all."

John was making reference to the small vegetable garden that he and his wife maintained in back of the cabin. In it, they grew tomatoes, potatoes, and almost anything else that could be raised in the tough Adirondack soil. It wasn't easy, but then again, they were fairly determined.

"Yup, a bit of rain will do us good. It keeps down the number of hikers. They don't like the thought of walking in the rain, so they usually just shack up in a lean-to somewhere 'till it stops. Makes it nice and quiet back here, at least for a little while."

I leaned back in my chair while John spoke, listening to his bit of anti-hiker sentiment. I had heard it before, and I could understand where most of it came from. After so many break-ins, and so much time spent repairing senseless damage to lean-tos and outhouses, John had had enough. Not that he was antagonistic towards any one individual or group. On the contrary, he was extremely helpful and friendly whenever assistance was needed. But he often commented on the types of people in the woods "these days," and how they had gone downhill over the past twenty years.

John was in a unique position to make such observations, as he had literally been living back there longer than I had been alive. Prior to his seven years at the interior rangers' station at West Canada Lakes, he had spent thirteen years at the cabin on Cedar Lakes, and an additional six years as the forest fire observer on Tomaney Mountain. Heaven only knows where he'd been before that. In other words, he had "been there," and I valued his opinions as much as I enjoyed listening to his stories.

It was hard to imagine some of the things that he passed on to me during those long afternoon sessions in front of the pot-bellied stove in his living room. For example, he told me that Cedar Lakes had once been just that, a collection of three distinct, separate lakes that had been merged into one large body of water by the construction of the Cedar Lakes dam. I really couldn't picture it until I came across a map that was produced prior to the dams' construction.

"We had about twenty or thirty folks helping us at different times as we built that thing," John reminisced. "Big project. And everyone working back there used to stay in the cabin with us. It was a bit bigger than this one," he said, glancing around his current abode. "We used to send out weekly shopping lists, and the state would reimburse us for food, but they wouldn't pay us for either cigarettes or beer, so we had to cheat a bit to get them."

This tweaked my curiosity. "What do you mean, John? How could you get that stuff if they wouldn't let you buy it?"

"Oh, it really wasn't much of a problem. Whenever we started to run low on our cigarette or beer supply, we'd just include 'peaches' on our shopping list. They'd pick up the contraband for us and call it peaches on our expense report. We got our beer and cigarettes, the construction crew was happy, and the folks down in the office (DEC) never knew the difference. The only thing that they ever said was that we sure went through a lot of peaches!"

I got quite a laugh out of that one, thinking about the recurrent item appearing on the shopping list.

While John recounted the story, Barb (John's wife) sat by, chuckling at the memories. She had lived at the cabin on Cedar Lakes as well, and often fell into the role of camp chef, preparing breakfast, lunch, and dinner for the crew of hungry workers. Along with her many talents, she possessed a sharp wit and sense of humor, and could trade jibes with the best of them. She was fun to be around, and I always enjoyed her company whenever she was at the cabin.

Barb visited on a fairly regular basis, even though the trip back into West Lake was quite long. However, these excursions were made easier by John's use of the many shortcuts and "water taxis" (boats) that he had hidden throughout the territory. John very seldom walked the normal "highway" trails that he maintained for the public on a daily basis. Instead, he preferred to travel via the interior trails that were hidden from the public. These abandoned paths were known only to the local hunters and fisherman, and still provided an effective means of transportation between the numerous lakes of the region.

Many of these hidden trails had once been part of the regions' trail system, which was much more extensive when the resources were more plentiful. The topographic maps that we used in the 1970s, for example, showed a trail leading from Cedar Lakes up to Twin Lakes, a few miles to the north. As often as I looked for a sign of the old route, I never could locate it.

I asked John about that particular stretch of trail, noting my inability to locate its source. "Nature reclaims things pretty darned fast around here," John replied. "About all you'll find is an occasional mark on a tree, and you'd probably have a tough time finding even that. It doesn't take long, once we stop cutting out the blowdown and knocking down the underbrush."

John showed me a map of the original trail system of the region, and I was amazed. I realized that what remained was only a small portion of the original pattern of main and feeder trails that surrounded many of the lakes and entered the West Canada Lakes Wilderness region from all sides. Many of them made stops at lakes that have, in all probability, not been visited by any human being in twenty to thirty years.

John's entire family was part of the backcountry scene at one time or another. John and Barb had three daughters, all of whom had an interest in the local territory. Debbie, his oldest daughter, served for several years as part of the trail crew, while Marge (the youngest) graduated valedictorian from the renowned State College of Forestry in Syracuse. The middle daughter, Marian, filled the position of Forest Fire Observer on Pillsbury Mountain, becoming the only female observer in our part of New York State. (As a matter of fact, she was my immediate successor on top of the mountain, and was able to make such major improvements on my efforts that I was a bit embarrassed to visit.)

John was fairly particular about the way in which he maintained the grounds around the cabin on West Lake, carefully grooming the grass around the cabin with his prized antique (but gas-powered) lawn mower. He always steered well clear of the massive fireplace which dominated the front yard, for fear of disturbing his "pets."

The fireplace had been built by Adirondack French Louie, who had supposedly carried several garter snakes into the woods in order to eat the insects in his garden. Legend has it that the snakes that still inhabited the fireplace (John's pets) were direct descendants of those serpents, and they could often be seen on warm summer days as they sunned themselves on the heavy mantle rocks.

The front yard also sported an equipment rack on which John

kept a variety of oars and paddles. These were primarily relics from the past, as very few operational boats remained in the territory. John did maintain one rowboat in usable condition, which he'd use while making an occasional attempt at landing the lunker lake trout. As a matter of fact, the equipment rack also held two skeletal remains of fish jaws, which had been removed from a pair of obviously oversized lake trout. One of them was so big that it reminded me of a scene from "Jaws."

"Yeah, I put those up there just to make folks think a bit," he chuckled. "West Lake is the only one out here that's deep enough to hold lake trout, and the fishing used to be pretty good out here. But that was before the acid rain hit," he said sadly, reflecting on the change. "That pretty much wiped out everything."

"You used to be able to catch a lot of them out here," I asked?

"Oh, hell yes. Sometimes, after the end of the season, I'd look over the end of the dock out in front, and I'd see 'em lined up in the water, some of 'em looked as big as submarines. It was almost like they knew the season was over and you couldn't take them anymore. It hardly seemed fair."

John seldom moved very fast as he went about his business. The truth of the matter was that there was very little which required urgent action, and John was quite good at conserving energy. But he was extremely good at doing his job, which involved maintaining the trails and facilities surrounding the West Canada Lakes area.

On at least one occasion, however, I did get to see John operating at high speed; he could still motor down the trail with the best of them. It was a warm, muggy day in July, and John had been doing battle with the beavers that had been flooding out the marsh in back of the station. This was an ongoing war, and I didn't envy John's task. For as hard or as often as he tried to remove the sturdily constructed dams, the animals would return the following day, acting every bit the proverbial "busy beavers" as they patched and mended their construction. There was no doubt that John was on the losing side, and he was looking for an excuse to abandon his burden for a short spell.

Little did he realize that the ultimate summertime diversion had just arrived "en mass," and were holding court just a short distance from the cabin. Evidently, a group of eight or ten young women, accompanied by one man, had hiked up from the south, and had camped at the lean-to on West Canada Creek.

When John returned to his cabin, he encountered a couple of hikers who had passed by the lean-to within the hour, and reported to John that "a large group of college-aged girls were skinny-dipping in the creek," and wanted to know if that type of thing happened every day.

"No," replied John. "This is a first...and I'm not going to miss it!"

With that, John sped out the door, and made Olympic time as he sprinted down the 1.2 miles of trail that lead to the spectacle. (To this day, I still laugh at the thought of seeing dust clouds following John's heels as he flew over the dirt path.)

According to John, he arrived just a few minutes too late. I asked him about the episode later on that afternoon, as he sat in the front room of his cabin.

"It was too bad," he shook his head sadly. "Those hikers had been right. They had been skinny-dipping for most of the afternoon. But they stopped before I got there. As a matter of fact, they had just gotten out of the water and pulled their clothes on when I arrived. And to top it all off, I got there just in time to see the guy go skinny-dipping!"

Teaching Don the Ropes

"What are you doing?" I asked incredulously.

"Making myself a sandwich, I'm hungry, is there anything wrong with that?" came Don's response. He was sitting on the edge of the fireplace at the Beaver Pond lean-to, squeezing the contents of the plastic jelly dispenser onto a slice of crusty brown bread.

"No, of course not, it's just that I've never seen anyone make a tuna fish and grape jelly on rye before. Let me know how it tastes."

It was a rather unusual combination, and I really had no desire to try it myself. But then again, nothing was ever quite normal when I got together with Don. He was a good friend, but a most unusual individual. I never knew what to expect from him, and it kept life interesting.

I had met Don Black in my college days, and we had become close friends over the years. After graduation, I found that Don was one of the few people with whom I'd stayed in touch. We tried to see each other once in a while, especially since he lived just a few hours away, near Albany.

I was quite enthusiastic when Don called to ask if he could come along on an entire week-long patrol. I was always thrilled to "show off" my territory to friends, and I readily agreed to take him along. I was planning to hike in from Perkins Clearing during the week that he would be coming up, which was a relatively easy route. There wouldn't be single day that would be extremely long or arduous, which can quickly ruin a newcomer's ambitions.

Don was not a backpacker, and thus did not own a lot of the equipment that he'd need for the trip. Fortunately, his brother seemed to have done some trekking, and was willing to lend him some first-rate gear, including an expensive frameless pack and a goose-down sleeping bag. What equipment Don didn't have with him, I supplied from my personal storehouse.

Don could also be a little stubborn at times, and I hoped that this wouldn't cause problems for us once we got into the woods, although I felt fairly confident that, out here, he would listen to my suggestions.

Our hike into the woods was fairly uneventful, although it took about an hour longer than I was used to. It wasn't that Don was a slow hiker; in fact, he could set a pretty rapid pace on level ground. It was just that he couldn't walk and talk at the same time. Each time we'd begin a conversation, he'd stop to think about the topic before responding in his deliberate manner. I quickly learned not to ask questions unless we were sitting down for a rest.

Another reason for our late arrival was Don's fascination with beaver dams. He wanted to take pictures of as many of these structures as possible. There was nothing that I could do to convince him that, for the most part, one beaver dam looks pretty much like the next, unless, of course, if you're a beaver.

We arrived at Cedar Lakes lean-to #1 (next to the dam), and we set up camp in the empty shelter. There was nobody else in sight, as was the norm for a weekday evening. We spent the afternoon gathering firewood and trading stories from our school days. It was good having friends around. Even stubborn ones.

Later on that afternoon, the wind slowed down considerably, and the fish started rising to the surface of the lake. It looked like a perfect day to snag "the big one," and I enthusiastically hooked a worm onto my line and cast it into the narrow waters above the dam. I probably wouldn't catch anything, but I always enjoyed trying.

Don came down and stood nearby, watching my efforts while continuing our earlier conversation. I tried to keep up a running dialogue, although my attention was being diverted to the fishing line, which was being nibbled at by something below the surface. This didn't happen too often, as I was not a skilled angler, and I usually didn't spend too much time trying.

Don was in mid-sentence when I felt the sudden hit of the brook trout. Not overly hard, but hard enough to let me know that he had taken my bait. Yahoo, dinner! (I never was one of those folks who throw everything back. If I catch a fish, it's because I want to see it on my plate.)

As I had guessed, it was a brook trout. It measured in at about 12" in length, but I really couldn't say what it weighed. It was beautifully speckled along its length, which is characteristic of the species. I gave a yelp of excitement and turned to show it to Don, only to find that he had already disappeared in search of his own rod.

While I returned to the lean-to, Don tried casting into the same part of the lake where I'd taken my prize. Not to be outdone, he too was able to hook a trout that resembled mine in almost every characteristic.

What a day. Nice weather, good friends, and a couple of gorgeous trout to go along with dinner. It just couldn't get any better. I got out my frying pan and olive oil in preparation for the feast, the thought of which had my gastric juices flowing. I was in the process of heating up the pan when Don spoke:

"Don't fry mine, I'd rather have it poached or something."

"What?" I asked. "I only know one way to make trout back here, and that's fried in oil and covered in seasoned bread-crumbs. How are you going to poach a trout, anyway?"

"I don't know," came Don's response. "It's a lot healthier than frying. As a matter of fact, maybe I'll just boil it up to save time. I don't think it will taste any different." I turned to look at him, to see if he was kidding. He wasn't.

"Don you can't boil trout! It just doesn't work! You'll end up ruining the fish." It was useless. Don had made up his mind that he was going to have boiled trout, and there was apparently nothing that I could say to show him the absurdity of the idea.

While my fish was browning and sizzling in the pan, Don was cleaning out a coffee can that has been sitting inside the lean-to. He filled it with water and placed it on the fireplace grates above the flames. This was going to be fascinating, and I watched his moves with great interest.

It wasn't long before my trout was done, cooked to marvelous perfection and wafting sumptuous aromas into the air. (Every bear for miles around must have lifted his nose and taken notice of our campsite.) I sliced off a couple pieces of bread from my loaf, creating a truly fabulous sandwich. Ah yes, this was what it was all about.

By this time, the water in the coffee can had heated to a rolling boil, and Don began cooking. He held his trout by the tail, aimed downward, and dropped the fish directly into the water. It was a sad sight.

During the next five minutes, the fish went through about three or four metamorphoses, after which it was no longer recognizable as anything that could (or should) be eaten voluntarily. It had changed color and shape several times, ending up as an inflated white object with fins.

Adding to the oddness were the noises coming from the pot, as the now rigid fish bumped against the sides of the can while turning over and over in the churning water. It reminded me of the sounds made by a car driving on a flat tire, going "ka-thump, ka-thump, ka-thump" down the road. It was a strange sight, and even Don had to concede that boiling the fish was probably not a good idea. I agreed, and made him a pot of macaroni and cheese.

The following morning we broke camp and headed westward towards the middle of the territory. Don strolled off towards the outhouse while I packed up the rest of our gear. I didn't mind doing this, as I considered packing to be somewhat of a ritual. By packing the same things in the same places and in the same manner, I was able to quickly locate almost anything in my pack, which reduced my set-up time significantly.

Within thirty minutes, I had completely finished packing our belongings, getting water from the spring, and tidying-up the lean-to. I was ready to hit the trail, with one exception: where was Don? He couldn't still be in the outhouse, could he? I called up the hill and received back a muffled response that resonated from inside the tiny structure. He was still in there!

Anyone who has been inside of a well-used outhouse knows that it's probably not the place where you'd most like to take a leisurely break. Don had been up there for a good forty minutes. I just hoped that he hadn't fallen in, as there were limits to even the best of friendships.

Our hike to West Lake was filled with sunshine and good conversation, which, in turn, lengthened our hike once again, due to the many chat stops that we took along the way. It was an enjoyable afternoon, and before long we were rolling out our sleeping bags in the lean-to south of the caretaker's cabin on West Lake.

The weather was supposed to remain nice throughout the day before turning cloudy the following morning. That was okay with me, as I never really minded the rain, but I knew that Don would not appreciate hiking through it, even if it was not supposed to come down very hard. It was just one of those things that took some getting used to.

I arose quite early the following morning, noting the heavy

layer of clouds parked above. They weren't what you'd call "thunderboomers," as they just didn't have that threatening appearance. But they did look as though they could produce a significant amount of rain on short notice.

True to form, Don arose from the depths of his sleeping bag shortly before lunch. (I've taken the literary liberty of exaggerating this schedule a bit, however, Don was never known for being an early riser.) As a matter of fact, he often emerged from hibernation so late in the day that breakfast was a moot point, and he'd instead dive directly into lunch.

Rising from the floor, Don stretched lazily and cast a critical eye towards the overcast sky. He was apparently quite concerned about getting caught in the potential rain.

"You wouldn't happen to recall where my rain suit is packed, would you," he asked.

"Sure. It's in the upper left pocket of your pack. I put it there so that you could get at it quickly if it started raining. I even put your pack cover in the same pocket."

He seemed satisfied with my answer, and went about the business of making brunch, which consisted of some nondescript canned luncheon meat spread on saltine crackers. While he did this, I finished packing my pack and started assembling Don's gear. I knew that if I didn't do this, we could be there until rather late in the afternoon.

Well, we were finally ready to leave. We were only traveling about four miles that day, down to the Sampson Lake lean-to. However, I was itching to hit the trail, and was greatly relieved when Don returned from another thirty minute hiatus in the outhouse. How did he do it? Well, I suppose he had to!

As I filled my canteen, Don climbed into his rain suit. His full-body, plastic, non-breathing rain suit. The suit that he was going to wear on this hot, muggy July afternoon while hiking with a heavy pack. Not a good idea.

"Uh, Don, I really don't think that you want to wear that thing today," I commented. "You'll perspire so much that you'll get wetter than if you stood out in the rain."

Naturally, Don did not agree with my point of view. "It's going to rain, and I don't feel like getting caught in it," he argued. "It makes more sense to just put it on now, and then I won't have to worry about it later on."

"But Don, you don't even know if it's going to rain," I exclaimed. "And just between you and me, I don't wear rain gear at all unless it's coming down in buckets, 'cause I feel like I'm getting even wetter by just having the stuff on in the first place."

My argument made him consider the matter for a fleeting moment, and I detected the mental processing reflected in his eyes. Then, he rejected the idea, threw his pack onto his back, and prepared to hit the trail.

Oh well, I had tried.

The hike to Sampson Lake that afternoon went as expected. The temperature hovered in the high eighties, with the humidity zooming up towards the top of the scale. It was, in my mind, a great day for hanging out at a beach with a cold drink in hand. I noticed that I was continuously using my bandana to wipe away the sweat that was trickling down my face and chest.

The four miles of trail rolled by quickly, and we arrived at Sampson Lake in plenty of time to gather wood for an early supper. As I removed my pack and slung it into the front of the lean-to, I glanced back at my companion, who was following a short distance.

Poor Don; even from a distance, it was easy to tell that he had suffered along the way. As expected, he had quickly sweated through his clothing, and had drenched the entire inside of his rain gear. Drops of perspiration dripped steadily from inside the sleeves of his jacket, making rain-like noises as they fell onto the leaves below. It may have been my imagination, but I swore that I could hear a soft "squishing" sound from inside his hiking boots each time his feet met the ground. He was a sight.

Don pulled off his pack, laying it next to mine in the lean-to.

Then, pulling the rain jacket over his head, he exposed his blue cotton sweatshirt, which looked as though it had fallen into the lake. It was incapable of holding any additional water, as excess fluid was draining out of the bottom waistband and soaking into his shorts.

After a quick change of clothing, Don joined me in gathering wood for the fire, which would also be used to dry-out his water-logged apparel. I couldn't see how anything that wet was going to become dry enough to wear, but I couldn't blame him for wanting to try.

I finished setting-up the lean-to, and then went about the task of stacking up the wood near the fireplace for cooking and for our evening campfire. It was a process that I had fallen into the habit of doing. Even if I wasn't planning on starting my fire for several hours, I'd have it set for lighting quite early in the day. I always tried to arrange it so that just one match was need-ed to catch the entire fire.

While I was arranging the firewood, Don began stringing a length of wet rope between two trees that were about thirty feet apart. I hadn't a clue what the rope was for, although I did notice that it passed directly over the fireplace. Or perhaps I should say, through the fireplace, as the rope dropped down to within a foot or two of the cooking grates where we'd been preparing our food.

"Hey Don, what's the rope for," I asked as I leaned back from my work.

"I want to dry-out some of my clothes," was his reply, "espe-cially my sweatshirt. I want to wear it tomorrow and it's kind of wet. I figured I hang it over the fire for a while."

"Well, that might work, but you've got to raise your rope quite a bit. It's hanging so low that the weight of your sweatshirt alone will pull it right into the flames."

Don tugged on the end of his red beard, thinking about my comment. "No, I don't think so. That rope's pretty strong, I think it'll hold."

If it had been anyone else, I would have pursued the issue, as I knew what the outcome would be. But with Don, I didn't bother. I knew better.

Shortly after dinner, we finished clean-up and threw a few extra logs on the fire for our evening campfire. As I've often said, this was one of the most enjoyable times of the day for me, as I sat back on the front beam of the lean-to watching the flames grow.

Don stepped back into the lean-to and retrieved the bulky sodden mass that was his sweatshirt. Then, as promised, he heaved it over the thin cotton rope that was stretched over the fireplace. It didn't have a chance. Instead of holding the load, it sagged immediately onto the cooking grates, making a loud hissing noise as it came into contact with the super-heated metal.

Don removed the sweatshirt, and was actually able to raise the rope by an additional foot or so by tying the ends higher up the supporting trees. But the outcome wasn't much different, for when the wet clothing was put back on the line, it sunk to within a foot of the flames, where a gentle steam began rising from the fibers of the material.

I arose from my seat to help Don move the rope up even higher, as it was obviously way too low. Apparently, he wasn't interested, as he instead sat down in front of the fire and stoked the flames.

"Don, we'd better move your clothing up a bit more. They're still way too close to the flames, and I'm afraid they'll burn if we leave them there."

"No, let's wait, at least for a little while. That shirts pretty wet, and it'll need a lot of heat to dry out." There was a certain finality in Don's voice, as though he had been drying his clothes over a fire for years, and this set-up was just about perfect. There would be no mistakes this time around.

The two sleeves and cuffs hung closest to the flames, and were the first parts that actually caught on fire. Accompanied by a loud hissing sound, the flames crept up the material of the arms until they were half-way to the elbows. (Here we go again.)

"Uh, excuse me Don... your sweatshirt is on fire."

The sweatshirt was not a total write-off, although it was no longer a true long-sleeved garment. Doing my best to repress a well-deserved "I told you so," I draped the remainder of the shirt over the fireplace rocks, and was able to complete the process of drying it within a couple of hours. It was not pretty, but it could still be worn.

The following day we hiked out of the woods, and Don got set to leave for home. This week had been everything I had expected: strange, frustrating, and amusing. I'm sure that Don was leaving with one main thought in his mind: "That Larry is ok, but he sure has a different way of doing things."

After saying our goodbyes, I watched Don's car drive away down the dirt logging road that would take him back to Route 30. Then, I threw my own pack into my trunk, and started up the engine. I was heading towards Lake George.

—29—

A Hard Night at Whitehouse

By the time I had finished up my first two years in the West Canada Lakes Wilderness area, I had become quite comfortable with my surroundings. I enjoyed the schedule which Tom had arranged for me, as it allowed me to consistently get around to all parts of the territory. It was not terribly demanding, and seldom called for more than twelve miles of hiking in any given day.

Being a creature of habit, I guess I had gotten too used to this schedule, and was a bit surprised to find that my world had changed when I returned for my third season on the job. My territory had expanded to include a large chunk of "wilderness" south of Piseco, called the Silver Lakes Wilderness Area. It encompassed over twenty miles of the Northville-Lake Placid Trail, and passed through some extremely nice stretches of land.

Unfortunately, there was also a drive-in camping spot called Whitehouse. Not that Whitehouse was a particularly bad location or anything like that. As a matter of fact, it was home to a wonderful stretch of the West Branch of the Sacandaga River, where a lengthy suspension footbridge crossed over the rapids for the benefit of trail hikers. It was just that you could pull up and drop anchor. It could, at times, get crowded.

Unlike the West Canadas, I was familiar with this patrol route before I ever hiked it in uniform. I had passed through the region on two previous occasions while hiking from Northville up towards Lake Placid. My new patrol schedule consisted of a hike directly south from Route 8 in Piseco, reaching Upper Benson two days later. Then, I'd turn around and retrace my steps until I'd return to my car at the end of the week. There were no "loops" involved, because there were no side trails. It was just a down and back affair.

The very first time that I was scheduled to patrol this new route, I hit an unexpected snag. I had pulled my beat-up 1971 Oldsmobile over to the side of the road and was preparing to put on my official clothing, when a local sheriff's car pulled up behind me with its lights flashing.

Uh oh. What had I done? I hadn't been speeding, and I was legally parked. True, my car was completely rusted through and had very few remaining operational parts left on it, but it had passed inspection (by some miracle that I still cannot figure out), and wasn't currently violating any laws that I could think of. I was puzzled.

As I slid from behind the steering wheel, I caught a glimpse of myself in the rear view mirror. Aha, that must be it! My hair had gotten a bit long, my beard was way out of control, and I looked like an escaped convict from the state penitentiary. In my green uniform and green army-style hat, I could have passed for Fidel Castro. (Actually, when my beard reached its longest point of 6-8", a friendly group of campers at Spruce Lake nicknamed me the "Wilderness Rabbi.") If I'd been the deputy in the patrol car, I probably would've stopped to investigate me as well.

The officer stayed in his car for a minute or two while he copied my license plate number and called it into his station. Then, he got out of his car and approached my vehicle.

"Where are you heading?" were the first words out of the

deputy's mouth. It didn't sound good.

By this time, I had slipped my ranger uniform shirt over my tee shirt, and was buttoning up the front just as quickly as possible. If nothing else, I could look like an official escaped convict.

"Hi! My name's Larry and I patrol the backcountry trails for the DEC. I don't believe that we've had the chance to meet, officer...?" I extended my hand for a handshake, hoping to get his name. He didn't reciprocate, and I hoped that he wasn't going to try and ticket me for something.

I offered some further explanations of my job, and what I did for the state along the trails and campsites of the area. He didn't seem overly impressed, and returned to his squad car to gather additional information.

Well, I couldn't see the point of waiting for him to file an investigation report, so I set about the task of packing the rest of my pack and lacing up my boots. As I worked, I could feel the intense scrutiny that I was attracting from the officer, who was actually just trying to do his job properly. Meanwhile, I was trying to act just as official as officially possible, and was putting on parts of my official uniform that I'd never bothered wearing before. I was officially on duty, and placed my official radio on top of my official car in order to officially sign onto duty. It was quite a show.

"Pillsbury Mountain, this is 1051," I stated in a firm voice. "I'm at the trailhead on Route 8 in Piseco, about to start my patrol south towards Whitehouse. All conditions currently normal."

I can only guess what Marion Remias must have been thinking up in the tower. She must have thought that I'd "flown the coop," so to speak, as I never signed in like that. (Nobody else in the world could hear my radio, so I usually signed in with a casual "Hi, Marion; I'm walking down to West Lake today.")

Within a few minutes, the deputy stepped back out of his car and walked over to where I was completing my final preparations. He eyed my radio, which prompted me to explain that I used it to communicate with Pillsbury Mountain.

"Yes, I know," he replied. "I heard you sign in on my scanner."

It must have been terribly anticlimactic for him, as he was finding out that I was actually (in a small way) part of the law enforcement team. But he still had to get in some form of a warning, as it appeared to be ingrained in his personality.

Pointing to the rear plate of my car, which still carried New Jersey tags, he said seriously, "Well, at least get your car licensed in New York State, OK?"

I promised him that I would, and also promised him that I'd keep an eye out for anything suspicious that might happen while on patrol within his jurisdiction.

I decided to avoid that kind of hassle in the future by changing my route just a little bit. Whenever I was assigned to patrol the Silver Lakes area, which only happened about three times that summer, I'd start off by driving my car back to Whitehouse. I'd then don a daypack, hike the trail back to Piseco, and then retrace my steps to Whitehouse. It made for a lot more walking on the first and last days of my week, as I'd have to cover the entire stretch of trail twice. But I could use a daypack instead of carrying my whole load, and leave my full pack in the car at Whitehouse. It also allowed me the liberty of using my car to get out of the woods on the first and last nights of the week.

I learned quite quickly that Whitehouse was an unusual place to be camped, especially for a "wilderness" park ranger. Walking along the various paths that lined the river, it was not unusual to be passed on either side by motorcycles and dirt bikes, while children played baseball in the parking lot. Music blared out of portable jukeboxes, and people cooked elaborate picnic meals on huge grills. It reminded me of many of the state campgrounds, and I felt grossly out of place whenever I stayed there.

The addition of the Silver Lakes Wilderness area added some confusion to the paperwork I was supposed to submit regarding my activities on the job. My first visit to the Whitehouse campground showed me that it would be impossible for me to accumulate accurate data on the numbers of campers present, the duration of their stay, etc. There were just too many of them, and they were spread out over a vast, sprawling series of fields and woods. Instead, I decided to limit my administrative efforts to the qualitative forms, which asked for descriptions of the conditions of the various trails and facilities. That much I could do.

I also tried, for a while, anyway, to perform my official responsibilities of educating the public about safe camping procedures. It didn't work, at least not at Whitehouse. After all, it was really more of a city parking lot than a wild forest. I'm sure that everyone there knew a great deal more about staying safe inside a twenty-eight-foot camper than I did.

One small detail that folks did have to worry about while camping at Whitehouse was the local bear population. It was one of the few spots in the area where tent campers really did have to hang their food. (This was never a problem in the West Canadas.) I'd often show people how to select the right size tree, and how to get their food bags "up and out" from the tree trunk sufficiently to protect them from the nighttime snackers.

This was not always as easy as it sounds, as we did have some fairly creative bears in the area. I never got to see any of them climb up and retrieve a bag by pulling on the rope, but I did witness a "kamikaze bear." It would climb up above a poorly hung bag, and then lunge at it, often taking the bag and the attached branch to the ground with a loud thud. Quite a sight, I might add! And a real hit with the campers, although the folks who owned the food didn't usually appreciate it quite as much as the rest of us.

Although I had my car at Whitehouse, I very seldom drove anywhere. After all, my schedule called for me to actually camp there on those nights, so I really had to stay close by in the evening. And there wasn't that much to do in the metropolis of Wells, NY, where the dirt road to Whitehouse left Route 30. It was a sleepy little vacation town on the lake, and it didn't have an abundance of nightlife. So my normal evenings at Whitehouse consisted of an early dinner and a quiet fire in the most secluded campsite that I could find.

One notable exception to this rather uneventful routine happened quite unexpectedly. It was a Monday evening, and I had just hiked from Silver Lake back to Whitehouse, which is a beautiful walk through some fairly remote woods. I always enjoyed staying down at the Silver Lake lean-to, as it was a quiet spot that was used mainly by hikers moving up the Northville-Lake Placid Trail.

I had just finished setting up my tent when I saw the green roof of Rick Miller's truck bouncing down the dusty road. Yahoo, company! This was an unexpected pleasure, as I was not used to having visitors during the middle of the workweek.

Rick suggested that we head out to dinner, rather than cook something over the fire in the crowded campground. It sounded like an outstanding idea to me, as I had no real desire to eat the can of beef stew that was sitting in the trunk of my car. Somewhere in town there was a plate of cheeseburger and fries with my name on it. I was determined not to let it go to waste.

We packed up my belongings and tossed them into the trunk of my car, leaving only the tent behind at the campsite. I parked my vehicle next to the tent, to make it look as though somebody was "home." (Not that I didn't trust people; it was just that things did occasionally disappear.) Then, we jumped into Rick's truck and headed for town. Staying at Whitehouse did have its advantages after all!

We drove south on Route 30 for some time, ending up in Fort Plain, along the Mohawk River. It was a lengthy trip, although the good conversation made the time go by quickly. It was always fun to talk with fellow DEC colleagues, as we often compared notes and found that we had endured many of the same experiences in our trials and tribulations with the state.

We ended up at a very comfortable spot on a side street in Fort Plain called the Center Street Station. The sign out front read "a drinking establishment," which pretty much provided an accurate description of the place inside. It was done up like an old barn, with a brass bar and exposed wooden beams overhead. On that particular evening, it was just what the doctor ordered.

Rick and I slid onto a couple of bar stools at the counter and ordered our food. I was in heaven.

Sandwiches, salads, and fries were foods that just didn't appear on the menu when you lived out of a backpack for several weeks at a time, and I wolfed down a fairly large quantity of every-thing. We washed our meals down with a few bottles of good beer, which always seemed to taste that much better when con-sumed after a long day of hiking.

My original plan that evening had been to grab some dinner, and then head back to Whitehouse. However, it didn't quite work out that way. We somehow got pulled into an impromptu game of pool with some folks who Rick knew from town. They were very friendly people, and we ended up chatting for several hours while sipping on a few more beers.

Next, the party moved onto an outside patio, where we talked for quite a bit longer. We had a few more beers, and pos-sibly a few more beers. And maybe...well, I'd rather not draw this discussion out longer than necessary.

I really can't describe too many additional details of the evening, as my recollections end somewhere around 1:30 A.M. I do remember the words "last call" being spoken, and I vaguely recall the lengthy drive back to Whitehouse along the dark, winding road. (Thank heavens Rick was driving, he was in much better shape than I.)

We finally arrived back at the quiet campsite, and found my frost covered tent in the glare of the truck's headlight. I honest-ly could not say what time it was, only that it was much closer to morning than to midnight. Rick pulled his sleeping bag out of his truck, wisely deciding to sleep in the tent rather than to attempt the drive back to Kane Mountain.

Morning arrived entirely too early, and it took a considerable amount of effort and concentration to drag myself out of the sack. My mouth was dry, my eyes were red, and I had the "mother of all headaches" pounding away at my skull. I was hung-over, which was not a good way to start the workday.

Oh well, at that point there was not a lot that I could do about the previous evening. Rick repacked his sleeping bag and took off for home, while I started the chore of disassembling my tent. The campers surrounding me were already awake and making noise, noise of all types and volume, which did nothing to improve the throbbing inside my head.

I finished loading the last of my equipment into the trunk of my car and grabbed the small daypack which I'd carry on my patrol to the Piseco trailhead. I also picked up some of the forms that I was supposed to fill out describing the land use in and around Whitehouse. I really didn't feel like doing paperwork that morning, but at least my administrative duties would allow me to sit down for a while longer before starting my hike.

I wandered over to the footbridge and climbed down onto some of the rocks exposed in the middle of the river. Stretching out on the warm (albeit hard) surface, I unfolded some of the official documents that I was to complete.

After some time, I forced myself to take pen in hand and complete my assigned task. But it wasn't easy. I didn't have any real data, as I hadn't interviewed anyone while I was there. And I couldn't compile any long-term statistics on the place, since I had only patrolled there a couple of times the entire year.

Finally, I turned to the very last page of the package, still without having documented a single useful piece of information. My tired eyes tracked down the page until they got to the very last question, which read "Summary of Conditions at Site."

This one, I knew, I could answer. With tongue in cheek, I wrote. "Area is very crowded. Conditions were not good last night. Camping here really gives me a headache!"

—30—

Campsite Bears

"Help! Come immediately! Bear in campsite number 7."

It was a rather ominous sounding note, hastily scrawled on the back of a crumpled-up piece of paper that was tacked to the campsite ranger's door.

It was very seldom that I ever stayed in a state-run campsite, as my territory was so far back into the woods. However, on this particular evening, I had decided to get an early start on the work week by camping nearby the trailhead, at the Lewey Lake Campground.

Lewey Lake itself is a beautiful combination of water, white sand beach, and tent sites, which are comfortably situated under cool birch and beech trees. However, the area is also plentiful with *Ursus Americanus*, commonly known as the black bear. As a matter of fact, there were so many campsite regulars among the bear population at that time that the campsite employees had actually given them names: Sidney, Jonathan, Malcolm, and Pigpen seemed to be their favorites.

As any wildlife watcher knows, black bears are less danger-ous than their relatives, especially the grizzly bears found in the

American west. However, they must still be regarded as danger-ous, and must be respected as such; a black bear can become aggressive on short notice, and is capable of breaking a man's arm or leg with one quick swipe of its paw. I personally gave them a large amount of leeway whenever I encountered one on the trail.

Campsites in the Adirondacks did seem to draw these curious creatures for one very obvious reason: food. Bears are natural foragers, ambling about in search of berries, nuts, and other assorted snacks. Nature, however, does not provide such delec-tables as hamburgers, steaks, and cupcakes, so the bears come to the campers to do their shopping.

This particular bear was called Malcolm, and he had lived in the woods near the campground for several years, feeding off the generosity (offered or not) of the campers. Malcolm could usually beg enough food from the visitors to stop him from engaging in unwanted pillaging. However, on this particular evening, he must have been extra hungry, because he was in the process of consuming a family's entire weeks worth of groceries when the distress signal made it to the ranger's cabin.

As neither of the campsite's two rangers were in, things real-ly became interesting. Ken had the day off, and Bob was working on the other side of the lake. By coincidence, Ken had not gone home, opting to remain on-site during his day off. He was relax-ing with some friends, enjoying a beer or two, or three, or four. By the time Ken made it back to the cabin, which was shortly after the distress call arrived, he was feeling no pain.

But, being the diligent, hard-working ranger that he was, he pulled on a well-worn uniform and headed towards campsite 7, which was just a short distance down the road.

It was a truly bizarre scene, with an entire family perched precariously on top of a gleaming new Winnebago. Below, Malcolm was clearly in bear heaven, chowing down on a wide variety of savory supermarket selections. He hardly seemed to acknowledge Ken, who proceeded to stride rather unsteadily up to his side, hiccupping occasionally.

Ken was not an especially large fellow, nor was he any braver than any of the other park employees. However, on this particular evening, he was operating without fear, as well as without several of his other faculties. As campers in the surrounding sites watched with mouths opened, Ken scowled un-approvingly at the munching bear from a distance of barely three feet.

"Damn it, Malcolm, what the hell do you think you're doing," he hollered at the top of his lungs.

"You know you're not supposed to be out here before dark. If I told you once, I've told you a hundred times, STAY AWAY from the campsites during daylight. If I have to come back over here one more time, you'll be sorry for the rest of your life. Now go!"

With that final command, Ken turned smartly on his heels and started marching back towards his hut, while Malcolm turned right, and headed back into the woods.

It wasn't until the next morning, when a rather groggy Ken awoke with some foggy memories of the previous evening that he realized what had transpired. From what I heard later, he swore off beer for the remainder of the summer. And, for several weeks, scores of campers were asking where they kept the bears locked up during the day!

Confrontations between bears and campers can get ugly, although I have personally seen the abuse doled out from both sides of the battle lines. I once witnessed a senior citizen cooking her steak on the grill, when Jonathan galumphed over to her, sniffing the grill-top with his anticipating nose. Jonathan was a yearling at the time, and probably weighed somewhere between 200-250 pounds. His silver-haired competitor would have tipped the scale at about 95 pounds, soaking wet.

What happened next boggled my mind. The elderly woman, rather than give up her soon-to-be-ready meal, quickly reached behind her and grabbed a garbage can lid. Then, with a quick downward thrust worthy of an experienced blacksmith, she brought the lid down with a resounding "clang" over the bear's head.

The woman seemed to realize immediately what she'd done, and took an involuntary step backwards. The puzzled bear, who was unaffected by this minor interruption, shot alternating glances at the steak and the camper, before deciding that it just wasn't worth the effort. With a final incredulous glare at the woman, he moseyed off towards wherever it is bears mosey, in search of an easier mark.

—31—

Lean–To Living

I love staying in lean-tos. I really do. And there's something about an Adirondack lean-to that's different from any other lean-to in any other park. There's a certain feel about it that's so real, so tangible, that almost has a personality of its own.

In many parts of the Adirondacks, the number of hiking parties far exceeds the number of available lean-to space. In those areas, some interesting arrangements (or perhaps they should be called strategies?) may be observed as the would-be inhabitants carefully arrange their hiking times to arrive as early in the day as possible in order to secure a spot. However, this doesn't always work, especially if a large group of campers decides to stay for more than one night. And, unfortunately, reservations are not accepted.

Thank heavens the West Canada Lakes area was never so populated. With the exception of Labor Day weekend or the Fourth of July, most of the lean-tos were available most of the time. You could literally take your pick of the litter.

By comparison to most wilderness areas, the lean-tos located in our region were relatively old. Many of them dated back to the

1950s and 1960s. This was confirmed by the various dates and inscriptions that had been carved and scrawled into the old logs throughout the years. They were sturdily built structures, with a fair amount of fibrous materials stuffed between the timbers to cut off the draft in windy weather. They were also quite roomy, especially the older ones, which often exceeded eight feet to the top of the inside roof. It was not unusual to find a family of barn swallows nesting on top of the upper beam.

I always preferred the older lean-tos over the newer models. It wasn't just the extra room that I enjoyed; it was also their unique character. Some of the really old versions had cedar shingles with lichens covering the entire surface of the wood, giving them a life-like appearance. At one point, the Beaver Pond lean-to actually had a few small red maple saplings sprouting from the lower slope of its roof! However, some passer-by must have thought that that was a bit much, for I found them torn out before they had started to reach any real size.

Older lean-tos also seemed to have more "stuff" in and around them. Stuff is a collective term for any and all materials carried into the woods, whether logically or illogically, for any purpose connected with camping, cooking, eating, sleeping, fishing, illuminating, etc., and which is then left at that site for all eternity.

They often contained a variety of cooking utensils, including pots, pans, coffee pots, and odd pieces of silverware. It was not always clean, but then again, who cared back there? If you needed it, you'd clean it, and then leave it there for the next person.

Some lean-tos even had parts of heavy cast iron wood-burning stoves that had been there since they were flown in years ago prior to the current land use regulations. These were unusable as stoves, but often made convenient lids to cover the fire at night, thus preserving a good base of coals for cooking breakfast. Some of the old-timers used to tell me about how they'd walk back in there in January and seal up the front of the lean-tos using plastic and bedspreads. Then, they'd fire up the woodstove inside the lean-to until it was toasty warm.

Some of these same old-timers often complained to me about the lack of consideration shown by the following generations of campers. In their day, it was considered to be negligence if you departed a lean-to without making certain that it had a complete stock of food on the shelves and dry wood under the eaves, so that someone in trouble could survive there for a couple of days. To some degree, folks still did this in the West Canadas, although I sometimes suspected that it was born out of a desire to get rid of excess supplies prior to the final walk out.

Stocking the lean-to with dry kindling was a different matter altogether. It often upset me as much as it did the old-timers if there was none to be found, as I was a firm believer in providing dry wood for the next camper, at least enough to get a decent blaze going, anyway. But all too often, I'd arrive at a lean-to in the middle of a very rainy day, only to find it totally devoid of all combustible material. On one particular occasion, I became so perturbed that I spent a full hour collecting wood prior to leaving the campsite. I actually stocked the entire back wall of the lean-to with wood, and then left a note asking people to be considerate to the next user by doing the same.

I returned later in the week to find a completely bare structure. Not one stick was left. I hope they burned their dinners!

I realize that I've been extolling the virtues of these three-sided shelters for quite a while here without mentioning any of the drawbacks. While the negatives are few, they certainly can present themselves in the form of pesky nuisances. And the worst of these, by far, is the common mosquito.

Anyone who has ever camped in the Adirondacks in May, June, or July, knows what it's like. It's 9:00 P.M., and you've finished cleaning up the dishes. There's a beautiful sunset over the lake, and you've thoroughly enjoyed talking with your friends around the campfire. You crawl into the lean-to, snuggle down into your sleeping bag, and shut your eyes. Then...BUUUUZZZZZZZZ!!!

It sounds like an old World War II bomber coming in from a long ways off, growing louder and louder as it approaches. Then it's joined by a second, and then a third. And there's no escape.

During the worst months, campers would often pitch a tent just to get away from them. But this, too, could cause a problem, as some folks wanted to "have their cake and eat it too"; they'd actually pitch their tent inside the lean-to! (Why bother?) However, this was actually against the regulations, and I tried to enforce it whenever possible.

Lean-tos also presented a unique opportunity for the inhabitants to improve, modify, or decorate them. After all, it was very seldom that anyone was there to keep an eye on them. I usually passed each shelter only once a week, and there were a few that I saw only once or twice per year. Now that's what I'd call unsupervised camping.

I was told of a group of "hippies" who, during the late 1960s, hiked into the lean-to at Cedar River Flow, which marked the extreme northern edge of my territory. Evidently, they spent a raucous weekend partying in the lean-to, during which the rangers received word of drug use and some rather unusual behavior. Deciding to check it out for themselves, they walked in and found that the rowdy group had become bored with the color of the lean-to. The new color scheme (after their paint job) featured alternating yellow, purple, and green logs, capped by an orange roof. The structure could not be repaired, and had to be destroyed.

I personally never came upon anything closely resembling this incident, although I did observe some cases of "humorous improvisation." I arrived at Sampson Lake at the end of a weekend one August morning, and found that the previous tenant had brought in a canine partner. (I determined this, unfortunately, from the empty dog food cans left in the fireplace.) I could also tell that the dog had led a pampered existence; its owner had built a pooch-sized extension onto the end of the lean-to, to ensure that Fido was comfortable during their stay!

However, it was the lean-to on Third Cedar Lake (which was truly ancient) that had one of the most unique added features that I'd ever seen in the backwoods. One long-time visitor with an unusual sense of humor had taken the time and effort to carry a 120-volt electrical outlet, complete with socket and outer plate, into the woods. They then used a couple of shiny new Phillips head screws to affix it solidly between the logs of the side wall of the lean-to. I'm sure many a visitor did double and triple takes upon seeing that one!

Then, just when I thought that I'd seen the epitome of zaniness, someone else built upon that idea by carrying in a small portable electric fan, which they promptly plugged into the socket. It's probably still back there today, sitting quietly outside the lean-to with the rest of the "stuff."

—32—

Mental Snapshots

I had always known that I was lucky to work in such a magnificent place as the Adirondack Park. It was something I reflected on from time to time, as I went about my appointed rounds. I once knew a fellow ranger from another district who became jaded after a while, he was so used to the scenery. This was something I promised myself I would never allow to happen to me.

Sometimes this was difficult, as the daily treks were often arduous ordeals. Covering twelve to fifteen miles over rocky, muddy terrain could be tiring, especially if done during the midst of a driving rainstorm. These types of days tested your stamina, and made you think only of reaching your destination and preparing a comfortable campsite. The little things, such as the way the raindrops beaded-up on the ferns, were often lost in the hustle.

I found that my ability to enjoy the scenery was directly linked to my willingness to stop and carefully observe my surroundings. By doing this, I was constantly discovering new colors and patterns in plants and animals that had been around for years. For example, the beautiful yellow stripe on the back of the Marsh sparrow's head. I noticed it for the first time while sitting down for a quick snack on the shore of the Whitney Lake. When I tossed some breadcrumbs to attract a few birds, I noticed that they all had the same markings. Funny, but I never noticed them before.

Of course, every once in a while, you'd come across a scene that required no real powers of observation. These picturesque settings jumped out at you, and were capable of making even the most time-conscious hiker stop and stare.

Whether caused by the color of the skies, the foliage, or a friendly creature caught in an unusual pose, the result for me was always the same. I made it a point to try and take mental snapshots, which I could carry with me forever. I carried no camera, so an image in my memory would have to suffice.

Several of these pictures are etched deeper and more vividly than the best color photographs. On one occasion, I sat on the sandy eastern shore of South Lake, looking at the western sky. Dusk was approaching, and the bottom half of the sun was starting to disappear over a hill at the far end of the lake. Mount St. Helens had exploded just a few months earlier, which provided a full month of ruby-red sunsets. But this one surpassed any that I'd seen that summer.

As I watched, the sky continued to turn a deeper shade of red, becoming a violet-rose color where the distant hills met the sky. In the background, I listened to a song sparrow calling from its nest in a nearby spruce tree. The wind had increased to a steady breeze, and was pushing some light clouds across the color-palette sky.

I was transfixed, staring at this visual treasure, when a single, solitary goose passed rapidly overhead, flying west into the sunset. I watched him for several minutes as he became smaller and smaller, until finally appearing as a mere dot in front of the last vestige of sun. It was a beautiful, wild, and lonely scene which I shall never forget.

Sometimes these gems of nature were less spectacular in appearance, although equally striking for other reasons. One cold damp day, I found myself on the western shore of Pillsbury Lake taking some time out to refill a canteen. I was in no particular hurry, as it was still fairly early in the day, and I had but a few miles left to go.

Pillsbury Lake is a long, narrow body of water that has many finger-like bays and inlets. While the lake itself measures over a mile in length, it is only a few hundred yards wide; hence, the opposite shoreline is quite close.

As I headed down the slope towards the lake, the icy wind made it feel more like early November than late September. The sky was a jumble of dark grey and black clouds that were stacked on top of each other. They looked as though they could open up at any time.

My prognostication was correct. Within the next few minutes, it began to snow. Soon, the air was filled with masses of tiny, icy flakes. The wind was blowing so hard that the flakes traveled horizontally across the surface of the water. It was the first snowfall of the year, so the white crystals contrasted sharply with the dark green hues of the spruce and hemlocks which sur-rounded the lake. As I watched, the driving storm increased in intensity, while the visibility decreased quickly. The view across the lake was becoming more obscured, as though a heavy fog had descended upon the water.

Then, through the veil of the wind-driven snow, I watched in fascination as a single white-tailed doe stepped out onto the opposite shore. She lowered her head into the vegetation that lined the rocky contour of the lake, apparently taking an unhur-ried drink of water. It was a magnificent scene that combined the stark, harsh solitude of the wilderness with the dignified pres-ence of the deer.

I stood there for several minutes, watching through the haze while the ice bit into my cheeks. I wished that I'd had a camera with me, but I knew that I'd never forget the scene.

Then, as quickly as the doe appeared, she turned away into the depths of the woods and was gone.

—33—

Food

I like to eat. I always have. As a matter of fact, I'm rather interested in the entire process of food selection, preparation, and consumption. But mostly, I like to eat!

The task of feeding oneself in the back woods can be an interesting proposition. There are as many types of foods to carry and methods of preparation as there are hikers. I know because, as I said, I'm fascinated with the stuff. I always enjoyed watching campers as they went about their daily meal preparation rituals.

At first glance, it would seem like a lost cause. After all, items such as refrigerators, ovens, or food processors are hard to find at most lean-tos, and don't even think about a microwave. Utensils are limited to those time-tested pots, pans, and spatulas that will fit into the limited space in your pack. Then, to top it all off, the list of ingredients must be limited to those foods that won't melt or turn green within the first twelve hours of arrival. It's a challenge.

However, there is one saving grace, which is that anything cooked halfway decently tastes good around the campfire. This is something that I've never been able to figure out, although I know it to be true. I once had a hiker from the Albany area tell me that he enjoyed a particular stew so much that he tried to re-create the dish back at home. Evidently, it came out so badly that even his faithful dog wouldn't touch it.

Over the years, I developed a staple version of my favorite dish (enjoyed at least once a week), which I dubbed "Larry's DEC Stew." And, after fifteen years of silence, I've decided to release my secret recipe.

Many of the items listed as base ingredients are extremely inexpensive and easy to find in any local supermarket.

Base ingredients:

— $1^1/_2$ quarts of water in a 2-quart cook pot
— 2-3 packages Lipton Cup-of-Soup, onion flavored, or experiment with others
— Soup Starter vegetables, or other dehydrated veggies, may include carrots, peppers, peas, corn, or any other such stuff
— 1 package dried noodles. I prefer Ramen noodles, but do not use the seasoning that comes with these packages
— pepperoni, sliced $^1/_2$ " thick, then quartered
— hard rye bread, cubed and tossed in
— cheddar cheese, cut into cubes and stirred in

Optional additions:

— dandelion leaves, only if fresh, before flowering
— several crayfish, 3" in length or larger
— etc. (anything goes!)

Now for the important part: how to put this together in one delicious pot!

First of all, I use only one pot, a two-quart cook pot, to assemble everything. Why a two-quart cook pot, you might ask? Well, actually, it's the only one that I own. Everything that I cook comes out of that one bowl, which I stir using the only utensil that I carry; a large metal tablespoon. I've chosen not to expand to additional pieces of hardware due to my dislike of dishwashing.

Fill the pot about ³/₄ full with cold water. Spring water is best, of course, but lake water will do, since the boiling should kill off any of the nasty microorganisms, such as Giardia, that may potentially reside in the water.

Place the pot on top of the fireplace grates and heat until the water is warm. Remove from the fire, and stir in the Cup of Soup packages and the Soup Starter vegetables (or other dehydrated veggies). Keep in mind that some of these dried morsels will take some time to re-hydrate, and that it's far better to err on the side of overcooking.

Another tip that I've picked up over the years is that I never wash the outside of the cook pot. It's as black as black can get, and I'll vigorously defend it from any well-intentioned clean freak who wants to see everything looking bright and shiny. Everything cooks so much faster with blackened pots, and since I only eat from the inside (which I do wash), I really can't see what the difference is. Remember, black!

The water should reach boiling, with the seasonings working their way into the veggies, which should start softening as they cook. Within a few minutes after the water reaches a rolling boil, add the Ramen noodles, stirring them until they separate and become soft. Then, after waiting an additional minute or so (while the noodles cook), stir in the pepperoni chunks, ensuring that they are evenly distributed throughout the pot. These will add flavor to the entire dish, and really help to spice up the meal. (Try not to munch on too much of it while you're slicing it up for the stew!)

After the stew has been boiling for at least 5-10 minutes, remove from the heat and add the chunks of rye bread. The harder the bread, the better it is for the stew. I used to purchase mine at a local cheese store that sold a variety that resembled granite, and would hold up for several weeks in my pack.

Finally, as an added touch, I'd take my cheddar cheese cubes and stir them in, watching them melt slowly into the stew. I found that white cheddar seemed to hold up in my pack better than the orange variety (although that may have been a personal bias), and the sharper cheeses tended to last longer than their milder counterparts. And once again, the cheese added a real exclamation point to the rest of the meal, and was well worth the added weight to my food bag.

Before chowing down, there are a few optional ingredients that may be added to this culinary delight. The dandelion greens which are mentioned can be cut up and added midway through cooking. They can be fairly tasty, although they should be gathered long before they start to flower to ensure that they are tender.

The crayfish were also a tasty addition, although many people turn up their noses at the thought of using this ingredient. I preferred collecting a few larger crayfish earlier in the day, finding them crawling around the rocks near the edge of the lake. I'd sauté the tails ahead of time, using a few tablespoons of squeeze-type liquid margarine in the bottom of my pot. And, while only the tails are edible, I'd make use of the entire body as well by adding it to the stew while the dish simmered. After removing the pot from the fire, I'd remove the crayfish "parts" and discard them, adding the succulent sautéed tails back in during the final mixing.

As you might imagine, there are countless variations on this theme, and I often tried using different varieties of vegetables, noodles, and dried meats in order to add some variety to the menu.

Oh, by the way, this dish was called DEC stew primarily because it was a hodgepodge of just about everything, but wasn't truly committed to much of anything.

In conclusion, I'd like to offer one last suggestion regarding DEC stew. It does taste great when served in a lean-to after a hard day of hiking and climbing in the Adirondacks. But don't try this one at home, as it loses something in the translation.

—34—

Through–Hikers

I recently looked up the word "hike" in a very old version of the Webster's New World Dictionary, and noticed two items of interest. The first of these was the definition itself, which was, "a long walk, especially in the country or woods." The other observation I made was that the word "hike" was followed immediately by the word "hilarious," which tends to describe all hikers, at one time or another.

I find that, in general, hikers are easy to categorize. At the very bottom (or top?) of the family tree of hikers, I've always placed the local campers and hunters. These are friendly folks who can be found at the same lean-to or tent-site every year, decade after decade. If you ask them why they return to that same spot, they'll tell you that where their fathers used to bring them. They're always helpful, and can usually be counted on to supply a hard working ranger (that's me) with an occasional hot dog and cup of coffee.

A second group is the trekker-adventurer. Trekkers are a more mobile type of individual, usually a bit younger than the group mentioned above, and less likely to be a resident of the area.

They tend to travel more lightly and don't have spare hamburgers to share at the dinner table. They usually enter the woods for one to three days at a time, covering moderate distances. They like to distinguish themselves at the sign-in booths, where they'll enter such catchy names as "the Mountainmen," or "the Lewis and Clark Expedition." Hey—whatever works!

But, of all the groups, the most unusual, the most determined, and the most highly evolved species of the lot, I call them the "Through-hikers," and they are people with a mission. They go from point A to point B, and nothing will get in their way. Through-hikers are concerned with distance and time. Usually, this means a large amount of distance in a small amount of time.

The Adirondack Park has a long trail, called the Northville-Lake Placid Trail. As the name implies, the trail runs from Northville, on Route 30 in the Southern Adirondacks, to a point outside Lake Placid in the north. It is a scenic, 134-mile transit that cuts directly through the heart of the Adirondack Park, and is designed to wind its way through the park's lowlands, which includes some extremely remote territory.

The West Canada Lakes Wilderness area plays host to some thirty miles of the trail. This stretch is perhaps the most desolate and wild region of the entire trail. In the off season, it is often possible to hike for three days through this area without seeing another person.

Through-hikers love it. They pass through the entire wilderness area in a rapid, two-day, one-night assault, often covering twenty to thirty miles in a single day. This is amazing to me, as I usually lean toward the "ten miles and then go fishing" type of day. Unless something is chasing me, I just can't see the point in hurrying.

I once met a couple of gentlemen who were arriving at the lean-to at Cedar Lakes Dam after an arduous day of marathon trekking. They unpacked their things, rolled out their sleeping bags, and quickly started preparing some unidentifiable freeze-dried concoction. They introduced themselves as "Jim Short" and

"Jim Tall," as they both shared the same first name.

"Planning on doing the whole trail?" I asked, as I always liked to hear where people were heading.

"Yeah, we're going all the way to Placid," said the shorter of the two Jims. "We really don't have a choice, as our ride is picking us up there on Friday."

"Friday! You mean this Friday?" I nearly fell over backwards, as it was already Monday, which meant that they had just four days to cover the remaining eighty miles of trail. "Surely you jest!"

"No, that's how we usually do it," replied the taller Jim, who showed no outward signs of kidding about their schedule. "We left Northville on Saturday morning, and we've only got a week to see the whole trail. So we're pretty much on schedule."

I believe that my entire perception of the difference between through-hikers and local hunters/campers can be summed-up by an experience that I had on one sunny September day. It was early afternoon, and I had stopped near the shore of Mud Lake for a bite to eat. As usual, I looked for a spot about ten feet off the trail for a good resting place.

Perfect! A nice dry log that looked like a custom-made bench had fallen right next to a conveniently placed flat rock, which would make a fine table. The entire setting was partially hidden from the trail by a row of small spruce trees, allowing me a modicum of privacy while I devoured my peanut butter and jelly sandwich. Who could ask for more?

As I sat munching, a knot of through-hikers zoomed down the trail, heading west towards the caretaker's cabin on West Lake. There were three of them, although they passed by so quickly that my count may have been inaccurate. There was very little conversation as they scurried past. I was able to notice that their eyes were directed downward, towards the trail, in order to keep from tripping on the rocks that studded the path. None of them noticed me, sitting within spitting distance of their boots.

In their haste, I was invisible.

Nor did they notice the great blue heron, sitting on its nest fifty yards out on the lake. The heron watched them fly by, as did I. Instinctively, I clutched my sandwich, which I feared would be blown from my hands by the wind created by their passage.

It was a wonderful day, which I continued to enjoy as I washed down lunch with a few gulps of water. I was about ready to hit the trail again when I noticed another group of hikers approaching, once again in a westbound direction. Deciding to lay low again, I was curious to see how many people really looked off the trail while walking through the woods. I sat still, again partially camouflaged by the growth in front of me. Would I be seen?

As the two men drew near, moving at a leisurely pace, I recognized them as Mark Wells and Jeff Ransom. They were two "old timers" from Amsterdam, which is located just below the southern boundary of the park. They had both hunted and fished the area for years, and were now taking a jaunt back into their favorite territory.

This would be interesting. Both Mark and Jeff were experienced woodsmen with good powers of observation. But yet, as they moved closer and closer, they showed no signs of spotting me. Perhaps they were too lost in their conversation, which had turned towards the subject of football.

Finally, they reached my hidden perch. As with the group of through-hikers before them, they never looked sideways, never gave any sign that they had spotted me. In a way, I was disappointed, as I thought that this duo would've picked out a stationary squirrel at a hundred yards. I felt let down. Maybe there wasn't as big a difference between these two groups as I had imagined.

Then, just as the two passed by me, Mark turned his head ever so slightly and called out, "Nice day for a nap, huh Larry?"

Indeed it was!

35

Bugs

The West Canada Lakes wilderness area is an absolutely marvelous region that can only be described in superlative terms. It is huge in size and diversity, and it's one of the least utilized territories in the entire Adirondack Park. It has (in my unbiased opinion) the best lakes, trails, wildlife, and scenery of any single such area in the eastern United States.

Unfortunately, there is usually some bad that comes with the good. In the West Canadas, the "bad" was represented in the form of bugs. Biting bugs. Biting bugs of all shapes, colors, and sizes. Unwary visitors arrive blissfully ignorant of the onslaught that lays waiting as soon as they stand in one spot for more than a few minutes.

We have blackflies that clog our nostrils in the spring and deerflies which rip us apart limb from limb (OK, so I'm exaggerating slightly) later in the summer, and mosquitoes, boy oh boy do we have mosquitoes.

One of the things that always impressed me with the insect life in our neck of the woods was their intelligence. Or maybe it was their scheduling abilities. I'm absolutely positive that all of the biting insects that lived in the West Canadas had calendars and wristwatches, which they used to compare notes and schedule their predacious duties. Among the various species, no time of day or month of the year went uncovered.

The first few months of the ranger season, from April through early June, was always the toughest, due to the massive hatchings of the blackflies. They are highly capable of making life miserable. They swarm about in flocks of thousands, looking for anything mammalian. Being a mammal myself, I often found that I was the epicenter of their attention. Not a good place to be, unless you enjoy serving as the local version of a buffet.

There are a few advantages that we humans do enjoy over the blackflies, which makes doing battle just a little bit easier. They are unable to bite through clothing, which is a trick the mosquitoes have mastered quite well. Because of this minor deficiency in their design, they often land on hikers' clothing, and take an "overland" trip across a shirt or pair of shorts until they reach their desired arm or leg. They are also quite good at landing on hair, and then snuggling down into the scalp, where they'll eat their fill. Hats can help with this problem, although they can also simply serve to divert the crafty little devils down to your ears instead.

Another saving grace of the blackflies is that the actual bites don't really hurt or itch excessively. This is good news, since the average camper can receive literally hundreds of these nibbles during a springtime week in the woods. It's a given, so be prepared! The density of the blackfly population can get so high in wetland regions that, on certain cloudy mornings, it is impossible to determine whether or not it is raining while still inside the tent due to the shear number of flies bouncing off the sides of the tent, resembling the sound of raindrops.

I had a few strategies which I tried over time, some of which worked better than others. I tried a hat with a wide brim and insect netting that rolled down to cover my face and shoulders.

However, I found that it didn't take long before the flies landing on the outside of the meshing were finding their way inside. Soon, I was seeing these wonderfully inflated blackflies with colorful red abdomens prancing around in front of my eyes. I'm certain that they were laughing over my "bug-proof" hat. The hat was ditched after one short day of use.

Insect repellent, or "bug dope," is available in many varieties. Some of these worked better than others, and each hiker passing through seemed to have his or her own mixture of choice. Some were homemade concoctions containing powerfully scented ingredients, while others were scientifically prepared in laboratories specializing in bug taste buds.

Leighton Slack, my friend living in the camp at Perkins Clearing, once took me into his confidence about the ultimate bug repellent.

"You mix together a third of a cup of wintergreen, a third of a cup of skunk oil, and a third of a cup of pine tar oil. Heat it up in a pot for a bit, then let it sit for a couple of days," he confided. "You don't have to use a lot; a little bit will keep the flies away for a whole day."

I bet it would! It would also probably keep away friends, relatives, and spouses as well!

I'm not certain that bug dope works very well against blackflies; it just seems to make them search a little harder until they find an unprotected piece of skin they are able to eat to their hearts content.

There were times in early spring when these flies became so unbearable that I surrendered to my need to seek refuge. The only way to do this was to set up my tent and dive in, zipping up the screens behind me. If I performed this feat quickly, I could get into the tent accompanied by as few as ten or fifteen of the tiny predators, who were then "mine." They'd congregate on the screen door, trying to escape as though they knew that they were now on my turf. It was actually pleasurable to squash these few invaders before laying down for an unhassled, unbuzzed nap.

Fortunately, blackflies were fairly seasonal in our territory, and they became rather scarce by the second week of June. Coincidently, this was just about the time when the herds of mosquitoes began to emerge, and I often conjured up mental images of the two different families of bloodsuckers "relieving the watch," as one group departed and was replaced by the second. My other theory was that the mosquitoes had actually been there all along, it was just that there was no room available for flight with all the blackflies buzzing around. So, they sat waiting until it was their turn at the supper table!

Actually, the mosquitoes in the West Canada Lakes could've been worse, considering the amount of still water available in the area which they use for breeding. They also weren't especially big, although every once in a while you'd have a real helicopter of a skeeter land on you for refueling. And anyway, the bug dope that was available in the local stores did appear to work against them.

Many of the campers who stayed in the lean-tos tried to keep both the blackflies and the mosquitoes away by using smoke. This could come in the form of a smoky fire, or from a pipe, cigarette, or cigar. And it usually worked, especially for the mosquitoes. They just sort of disappeared whenever a good smoke filled the air. We all learned how to throw wet leaves on a blaze to send up clouds of grayish-blue haze. The only problem with this, of course, is that you ended up breathing in the stuff yourself. It's a well known fact (documented by thousands of years of scientific observation) that the smoke from a fire will always blow in your face, no matter which side of it you choose to sit on.

The mosquitoes hung around into July, when they were relieved by the deerflies. And that's when the pain really started. Deerflies are those large, buzzing objects with the spotted wings that will hang around your head until you let down your guard. Then, they'll pounce, usually on the head, ears, face, or neck. In military terms, they carry the largest payload; they're the B-52s of the fly world. A local fisherman once told me that he thought the deerflies hurt so much more than other flies when they attack because, "They take a chunk out of you when they bite." I really couldn't disagree.

Deerflies don't tend to swarm around in massive numbers. But that doesn't matter, it's a bit like having "just a few" razor-sharp daggers pointed at your skin, poised to strike. They hurt! And after getting bitten the first few times, most hikers are not willing to get bitten again. Personally, I find myself swatting my scalp every twenty to thirty seconds while walking the trails in July and August. Quite often, I'll nail one before it starts biting, which is cause for celebration. And as ridiculous as that sounds, most folks who I've hiked with in our area do pretty much the same thing, whether consciously or not.

Oddly enough, deerflies don't hang around for too long. As unpleasant as they are, they're gone by the middle of August. And then, for just one month, there is a relative peace in the air caused by the noticeable absence of biting flies. For one entire month, it is possible to relax and stretch out on the front of a lean-to without waving a shoo-fly bandana back and forth to disperse the billowing flocks of flying carnivores. From mid-August through early September, can be one of the nicest and most relaxed months to spend in the woods. But that's all the time you get; shortly thereafter the temperature begins to fall and the air starts taking on a pre-winter chill that keeps most hikers out.

Since leaving my position as a park ranger, I've often considered how rewarding it would be to discover the ultimate substance that repelled all bugs. A repellant that so disgusted them that they'd pack up their bags and move out for good. I wouldn't want it to be one of those super high-tech formulas, with the 27-syllable ingredients and the warning label that wraps six or eight times around the bottle. No, just something that works.

Who knows? Maybe it'd turn out to be something as simple as a common food, like a citrus peel. I really don't know. Perhaps I'd even revert to old Leighton's formula, although I'd still have to figure out how to get the skunk oil. That could be tricky, I'm not as fast as I used to be. And while I don't think of myself as an entrepreneur, I'd have to be guaranteed a pretty hefty sum of money to wrestle the oil out of a skunk.

Come to think of it, forget the whole idea. I'd rather build a smoky fire.

36

My Neighborhood

Living in one place for several years does have its advantages.

It didn't take me long to realize that life in the backcountry was much the same as it was in the city. By the time I had entered my second year on the job, I had become an accepted part of the trail through the West Canada Lakes region, and many return campers whom I'd met in the past stopped by to say hello and exchange pleasantries. It was nice to see these familiar faces as they made their annual trips into the woods, and they genuinely seemed pleased to see me passing by as well.

A few of our visitors made numerous ventures into Cedar Lakes and West Lake each summer. Most of these people were hard working individuals who had found our area to be the perfect place to kick back and relax. Some were single, with no schedules or family obligations to fulfill. Many of them became my friends, and I came to look for them as the weekends approached.

In addition to the friendship that these folks brought, they also carried in some more substantial commodities, and I was often the benefactor of their generosity. This may have had something to do with the fact that I didn't lose quite as much weight during my second and third years in the woods as I did during my first.

Joe Tamanik, a steelworker from Utica, was one of these folks. Joe had been introduced to the area years earlier, when his father used to fish the Cedar River Flow. He had become entranced by the beauty and solitude of the land, and had developed into a "regular." There were times when I thought that Joe spent as much time back there as I did.

Joe was about six feet tall, and of average build and strength. However, he worked in a large industrial recycling facility, and spent his days shoveling steel into large transportation bins. This was reflected in his forearms, which looked as though they were constructed of bundled piano cords. He was one of the few people who I'd come across who could easily beat me in arm wrestling. He was also a tireless hiker who could motor along the trails all day long without showing any signs of fatigue. I marveled at his stamina, as I had never possessed that kind of energy.

Joe's parents owned a successful bakery and deli in Utica. Because of this, he always seemed to have a pack full of good things to eat, including a wide variety of breads, pastries, and other items that seldom made it back into the woods. Many times, he claimed to have more than he could use, although I always felt that he brought along the extra goodies to share with the people he'd meet in the lean-tos during his numerous weekend excursions. I personally consumed many pounds of the delicious home-baked pastries, and always promised myself that I'd stop into their store if I made it to Utica.

If Joe was well known for "carrying the store" into the woods, then Anna was known for leaving it at home. Anna, from a small town south of Syracuse, NY, was another one of our faithful standbys, and it was not unusual to see her heading into the woods with her dog on two or three consecutive weekends.

Anna was a bit of a puzzle to me. She appeared to carry very little in the way of food, and I don't think that I ever witnessed her eat any of it. This was most unusual indeed, as she was a very large woman, and obviously needed a major source of nutrition in order to keep up her strength.

Anna became a familiar scene during my last summer in the woods, and could often be seen traipsing between the lean-tos on Cedars and West Lakes with her dog "Bowser." Bowser was a boxer who, through a combination of genetics and a lot of food, had grown to reach enormous proportions. And though quite affable, he looked like a force to be reckoned with.

I enjoyed the company of this friendly duo, although sharing a lean-to with them did have its drawbacks. Anna was an extremely friendly woman, however, she could also snore with the best of them, and I often found myself trying to get to sleep before her in order to avoid hearing the deep rumbles that she emitted every night.

Her canine partner didn't help matters either, as he'd often get up during the middle of the night to irrigate the ground around the campsite. Upon returning to the lean-to, he'd circle around the floorboards once or twice before curling up in a warm spot, which (to Bowser) meant any sleeping bag he could find in the dark. It was not unusual to be awakened at 2:00 A.M. by the sensation of a hundred pounds of panting pooch landing squarely on top of your vital organs. Not good.

Other friends on the trail included those hikers who traveled through much less frequently. Dick Murray was one of those. In fact, he was a bit like the Haley's Comet of hikers! Dick was the head groundskeeper for a private girls school somewhere in Connecticut, and his schedule kept him extremely busy for most of the year. However, he managed to shake loose for two weeks each July, when he'd assemble his pack and head for Northville. He'd only pass through once each year as he completed his annual 134-mile hike from Northville to Lake Placid.

Dick had been hiking for many years, and had spent quite a bit of time on the Appalachian Trail. It was from him that I heard a lot of the interesting stories that made me want to try "The Trail" myself, although the thought of covering twenty miles a day for months on end was just a bit too ambitious for my taste. But it was fun listening to his adventures, and I always tried to catch up with him whenever he passed through the West Canadas.

People like Joe, Anna, and Dick became my friends through-out the summer months on the trail, and I looked for them as often as possible. On occasion, we would agree to meet at a given lean-to on a weekend evening for a backwoods "party." Of course, they weren't real parties in the sense that you'd picture a Saturday night bash in town. No, it was just a few friends get-ting together for conversation, food, and fun.

Making new friends was one advantage to remaining in one area for several years. Another advantage was that you began to develop a reputation as the genuine authority on anything and everything that went on in that territory. By my third year in the woods, I began to meet people who knew me by name, even though I had never met them before. They had been told by their friends of "Ranger Larry," who could usually be found somewhere between West Lake and Cedar Lakes.

I always enjoyed talking to the younger hikers who passed through, and often found the very little ones enjoyed listening to tall tales around the campfire. I would usually oblige by recall-ing the time when a big bear poked his nose through my tent flaps, and I had to outwrestle him to save my food bag from being gobbled up. (The adults rolled their eyes skyward during my presentations, but the kids always looked enthralled!)

Some of the equipment that I carried also developed a repu-tation, which puzzled me. One item that many folks wanted to see was my coffee cup, which I had carried for several years. It was an official "Flintstones" mug, complete with pictures of Fred, Barney, and the rest of the crew from the popular television car-toon. This plastic mug had been through three years of camp-fires, and had been stained from entirely too much coffee. In addition, it had warped rather badly, and the handle was melted off from a particularly hot blaze. It was not a pretty sight. But for some strange reason, it had become a bit famous, and folks just wanted so see it.

Folks also thought I was an expert on the weather (for at least the next week or two), the fishing conditions (including where to find the big ones), and the precise distance (to the nearest mile) to the closest unoccupied lean-to. And while these duties were never listed in my original job description, it was clear that these good people just expected me to know.

I did sometimes try to give the impression that I moved through the woods without following the marked trails, as I often felt that this kept some of our rowdier campers in line. After all, if they never knew when or how I'd appear, they'd just assume that they couldn't get away with anything without me landing in their campsite.

Every once in a while this strategy backfired on me. I did, on one occasion, leave the Sampson Lake trail in order to take a roundabout route down to the lean-to. (The main trail goes past the lake on a high ridge, and a side trail descends several hundred yards to the lean-to below.) There was a large group of howling kids down there, making all kinds of noise, and I wanted to find out just what they were up to.

I took a direct route down to the waters edge, about a quarter mile before the shelter, and then began moving through the brush and undergrowth along the shoreline. However, I had no idea just how thick that undergrowth would become, and I soon found myself pushing with all my might to clear a path through the stickly spruce and fir saplings that blocked my route. It was rough going, and I moved along at a snail's pace.

Finally, after what seemed like an interminable period of time, I barged out into the small clearing in front of the lean-to. In front of me sat a small gathering of Boy Scouts, who stared at me wide-eyed as though they had expected a bear to emerge from the woods. Also sitting inside the lean-to was Anna, who had evidently made friends with the troop of young explorers, and Bowser, who was receiving a surplus of attention from all sides.

Before I had a chance to offer my greetings, a very young member of the group looked up at me in amazement, gazing at the branches and pine needles that must have covered my entire body. "Excuse me, Mister, but did you know that there's a trail that comes right down here to the lake? It's easy to find. I'll show you where it is!" His bright blue eyes and innocent expression rendered the comment all the more comical.

Anna was in hysterics, and was laughing so hard that she almost rolled off the front of the lean-to. "Yes, Larry," she cried, wiping away the tears that were streaming down her face, "if you ever want to find it, it's right over there! Just go past the side of the lean-to, turn left, and...!"

—37—

Leaving the Trail

Throughout each of my first two years as a wilderness park ranger, there was never any doubt in my mind that I wanted to return to the woods for an additional year. Even as the summer ended and fall approached, I was already thinking about the following April, when I'd once again make my home under the stars and inside the lean-tos of the Park.

By the time I was partially through my third year on the job, though, I realized that I had to try something else. I had to try something new, something different, and something that was going to take me someplace that I'd never been before. Little did I know how much my life was about to change!

My decision to apply to the U.S. Navy's Officer Candidate School came back approved sooner than I could have ever imagined. And while I was looking forward to my new assignment with great anticipation, I was also sorry to be leaving the woods that I had grown to love so much. This was especially true since I had no idea how many years it might be before I would have the chance to return. The final weeks of the season seemed to fly by faster than any other time in my life. It wasn't long before I found myself packing my final pack, heading into the woods for that one last week.

I decided to take along a few things that I had never carried into the woods before. For some reason, I brought along a head of iceberg lettuce, a red pepper, and a tomato. Not being a true backwoods gourmet, which is evidenced by the fact that I had survived the past three years on DEC stew, I decided that I wanted to have some real food with me just once. I also brought along a fancy box of crackers to go along with the cheddar cheese in my bag, as well as a bag of pancake mix and some maple syrup. It was going to be a "good eatin'" kind of week! (I also brought along a small flask of peppermint schnapps, although I'm sure that the State would have frowned upon that activity.)

The woods were fairly full of hikers that week, which was very unusual for early September. After spending a night at Cedar Lakes, I headed straight for John's cabin on West Lake, as I wanted to be able to visit with John and Barb for as long as possible. The talk had been that the state would be burning down the caretakers' cabin within the next year or two, and I realized that I would probably never see it again. It was a very sentimental trip.

I was surprised to find that most of the lean-tos were occupied by early Friday morning, which meant that those campers had been in the woods since Wednesday or Thursday. I decided to stay at the "West Lake #2" lean-to, which was immediately south of John and Barb's. (If you could push your way through the extremely thick spruce and hemlock trees, you'd find that the lean-to was actually less than a hundred feet from the side yard of the cabin.) I was joined there by a trio of hikers from New York City. Mike, Ellen, and John were first time visitors to our area, and were more than willing to have company. It turned out that they were avid climbers, and were making plans to visit the White Mountains within the next few weeks. Having many of the same interests, we had a lot to talk about.

One interesting phenomenon that I experienced during my

farewell patrol was my desire to shed my "officialness." I was not as careful about maintaining the professional aloofness that we were expected to portray. Because of this, I ended up becoming very well acquainted with several groups of hikers with whom I shared the various shelters that week. Mike and John invited me to join them on their climb of Mount Washington, which I had to decline due to prior obligations.

My diet also improved dramatically that final week, as I had taken along the extra provisions mentioned earlier. The first of these delicacies to go was the lettuce, tomato, and pepper, which I offered as my part of a communal feast with my new friends on West Lake. In return, they cooked up a large kettle of linguine with real (not dehydrated!) tomato sauce. I couldn't imagine carrying the weight of a large glass jar into the woods, although I'm glad that they did. We even had fresh parmesan cheese to spread over the top, which guaranteed this meal the title of "best backwoods feast ever." It may have been my imagination, but the following morning I felt certain that my pants felt just a little bit tighter around my waist!

I was glad to see that John was not overly busy that weekend, as I had wanted to spend some time talking with him before departing the territory. We had become good friends, and I knew that I would miss our lengthy conversations. During this last year in the woods, I had been the only wilderness park ranger assigned to our area, and John had nobody else to talk to, except for the hikers and daily phone conversations with his wife. It was a quiet place to live.

I decided to camp at the lean-to on South Lake that Sunday night, as I knew that I'd be heading back to Cedar Lakes for my final night as a ranger. South Lake would give me the opportunity to sit on the white sand beach and reflect on things, just within a short distance of John's cabin. There were still several groups of campers left in the woods at the end of the weekend, and I was joined on that particular evening by a nice young married couple from Connecticut as well as a solo hiker from Yonkers, north of New York City.

Over the years, I had met very few people with whom I did not enjoy sharing a roof. Unfortunately, this was one of those occasions. The lone fellow introduced himself as Phil, and he just seemed unhappy with life in general. Phil appeared to be in his early twenties, and had long brown hair that was pushed sideways across the top of his head. He seemed to harbor a grudge against all women, and made several comments degrading "their species" in general. He didn't seem overly blessed with gray matter. To make things worse, he carried a large handgun, which protruded ominously from the side of his pack.

Ah, yes, become a ranger, and meet all kinds of interesting people!

I spent a good part of the afternoon talking with the couple from Connecticut, who had been through our area a few years earlier. By coincidence, they were both named Chris, which made for one of the more confusing registration sign-ins that I had ever seen. It turned out that Chris (the husband) had proposed to Chris (the wife) at that very lean-to, which made this quite the sentimental return visit. They were both extremely pleasant folks who seemed more than willing to ignore our unusual shelter-mate.

We traded a lot of interesting hiking stories, with Chris and Chris referring to their times spent camping in the Berkshire Mountains, while I contributed some amusing anecdotes from my Adirondack chronicles. Phil chimed in occasionally, usually commenting about the stupidity of the various women that he'd known over the years. We finally tired of this, and began poking some subtle (and undetected) fun at our disgruntled guest.

"That's why I carry this gun," Phil stated. "This is a man's gun. It's a .357, and no woman is going to be able to shoot it the way I do. And that's important, because the black bears around here are really prolific."

"Yeah, and there are a lot of them, too," I replied, trying to add a little humor to the situation.

Phil turned his head to one side and looked at me, trying to understand my comment. Then, with the couple starting to giggle in the background, he nodded, and said seriously, "Yeah, yeah, I know what you mean." It was that kind of an afternoon.

Shortly before dinner time, I headed up to John's cabin, as I'd been invited to eat dinner with John and Barb. I knew that it would be the final time that I'd get to sit in the cabin and talk with John about the woods and the trails, about the pilots who used to land on the lakes, and about the price that he'd get for his otter pelts the coming winter. It was something in my life that I was going to miss, and I suspected that there would be no coming back.

It was a familiar scene in the cabin, staring at John's silhouetted form against the setting sun, which poured a rich orange light through the front window frames. His gray work pants were held up by an aging pair of suspenders, which looped over the top of his worn undershirt. John puffed on a cigarette, sending tendrils of smoke into the low light of the room.

"Sun's getting a bit lower in the skies these days," he commented, nodding towards the western end of the lake. "In midsummer, it'll set right down at the end of the lake. But by early September, she's moved all the way down over those rocks to the southwest. That means winter's coming. You can set your calendar by it."

I didn't say anything, preferring instead to look and listen to the sounds around me. In the silence, John seemed to read my mind.

"I know it seems like you'll be a long ways away from here," he said distantly, "but don't worry about it, everything will always be here, waiting for you if you ever decide to come back. And I don't mean the cabin, or the lean-tos, or even the same people. All of that's temporary. But these mountains and hills and lakes, they'll still be here, because there's nothing that we could do to change them if we wanted to. Heaven knows, I've seen a lot of attempts to make inroads into these woods, but none of them ever lasted too long."

I knew that John's words were true; that the woods would always be there, although it would be a sad day when I would no longer be able to stop by the cabin and trade stories of my life on the trails. It was just a natural part of my existence in the West Canada Lakes.

I stayed entirely too long that evening, enjoying John and Barb's company, and I ended up returning to the lean-to on South Lake in the dark.

The following morning, I packed up my things and headed up past the cabin for the last time. I didn't dwell there long, as I had said my goodbyes the previous evening. Just a short stop to look around the place one final time before heading eastward, towards Cedar Lakes and the final walk out to Perkins Clearing.

My final hike to Cedar Lakes passed by as in a dream. I lost track of time as I strolled along the familiar pathway, noticing things that I would have missed on normal patrol days. The thick green carpet of tall ferns that covered the floor of the woods had never looked as lush as it did that morning. The new sun, rising in the East, threw angled spears of light through the trees above. And the early fall leaves of the maple trees splattered bright red splashes against the blue sky.

On most days, I could cover the distance from West Lake to Cedar Lakes Dam in about two hours and fifteen minutes. However, on this particular occasion, I moved along quite slowly, feeling the ground crunching beneath my every footstep. I finally arrived at the lean-to after three hours of deliberate walking, savoring each dip and bend in the path. I had walked that stretch of trail so often that I felt as though I could walk it blindfolded, stepping over the rocks and tree roots that had become as much a part of me as the furniture in most people's homes. It would be difficult to forget.

I arrived at Cedar Lakes by early afternoon, and decided to stay at the old lean-to by the dam. It was where I had spent my very first night as a ranger, and it would be where I'd spend my last. And, like my first night in the woods, I would have company.

Pamela and Peggy were already installed in the lean-to when I poked my head around the corner. After talking with them for a short while, I discovered that they were from New York City, and had hiked quite a bit in the Adirondacks, although never making it into the West Canada Lakes before. They were both extremely friendly, and welcomed me to stay and share their shelter with them.

Pamela was jubilant about finding a territory where you didn't have to battle off either bears or other hikers to obtain a lean-to for the night. I don't think that she believed me when I told her that they could (at times) hike through the entire area without coming across another hiker.

"We just opened up a huge map of the entire Adirondack Park, and put our fingers down where it looked the most desolate," Pamela exclaimed. "This area looked positively barren, so we were really excited when we found out that it was accessible by a trail system."

The girls appeared to be in their early to mid-twenties and wanted to hear more about my experiences as a Wilderness Park Ranger.

"How many years have you been back here?" Peggy asked inquisitively. "And do you think you'll always work in this same region, or will they let you move into a new territory if you get bored?"

My explanation of my pending stint with the Navy drew incredulous stares from both of them. After all, what could be more different from stumping around the soggy turf of the Northville-Lake Placid Trail than joining the Navy? I could tell that they were both disappointed, as they sat staring at me with open mouths.

"You don't really want to do that, do you?" Pamela asked

doubtfully. "Why would you want to give all this up for a career on a ship? You'll have to spend all day saluting people and following orders. You must be crazy!"

During the next few hours, I learned several things about Pamela and Peggy. They were both "60s" kind of people who were into doing their own thing. They were also kind, gentle, and caring young women who seemed genuinely pained about seeing a park ranger "losing it" to go into the military. They spent several hours trying to convince me to change my mind, and even invited me to their house in the city so as to continue their pursuit.

My final night in the woods was one of my most pleasant ever, with a warm breeze blowing off the lake, gently stoking the flames below the grate. We made a large kettle of hot chocolate, which we drank interspersed with sips of the peppermint schnapps. It was a perfect evening.

As the sun went down, I went out to the edge of the lake, watching the fish jump at the small insects that floated on the surface. On most evenings, I'd grab my fishing rod and try my luck with the cautious brook trout that were rising to feed. But not tonight. This final sunset was for watching. And feeling, and smelling, and hearing. This one would have to last for a long, long time.

Sometime during the middle of the night, we were treated to a magnificent concert, provided by the loons down on the beaver pond. I stayed awake for several minutes listening to their songs, which triggered responses from other loons further down the lake. Their tones echoed off the hills surrounding the water, producing an eerie, solitary melody that I still recall as though it happened only yesterday.

I know it's impossible, but I'd like to think that the loons were saying goodbye, wishing me "fair winds and following seas" in my travels. Or maybe they, too, were telling me that I was crazy.

Afterword

I sat on the log in front of the new lean-to at Cedar Lakes, lost in my thoughts. It was a sentimental trip; a return to the past which sent my thoughts back to a different time.

The lean-to was a smaller version of the masterpiece that had stood by the dam during my tenure in the woods. The original model had lasted for thirty years before finally giving way to the elements. The replacement structure felt rather impersonal to me, being relatively new. However, I knew that it had been built almost ten years ago, and that many thousands of people had passed by since I last set foot here.

I never could have imagined it: where did the time go? It's been twenty-four years since I last stomped the trails as Park Ranger in the West Canada Lakes, although it still seems like yesterday.

To get to the lean-to, I had to cross over the Cedar Lake outlet on the rocks below the dam. The bridge that spanned the cement buttresses of the dam has been gone for a number of years, not to be replaced. The trout can now swim next to the retaining wall in complete safety, knowing that no stealthy fishermen can dangle their lines off of the wooden planks above. It was the same bridge I used to sit on after dinner to watch the sun set.

The woods have remained the same since I was last there. And yet, so much of me has changed. Many of my earlier dreams were fulfilled when my wonderful girlfriend said "yes" and became my wonderful wife. Patty and I were married about the same time as the new lean-to was built on Cedar Lakes. We now have a beautiful little girl who someday may enjoy walking along the same trails that her father did "back then." The land will still be there, only the faces will be different.

Looking around, I could still see some of my friends that I knew so well in those earlier days. A beaver swims down the lake from its home in the beaver pond, although I doubt that it's still the same one that I watched every night after dinner. He glides by en route for the dam, where he turns around and heads back towards his lodge. I see no signs of recognition from him as he pokes his head above the surface, warily watching me for any signs of aggression: I am now an unfamiliar sight in his territory.

Strolling along the north side of Cedar Lakes, it is getting harder and harder to see the remains of the old caretakers' cabin site by the side of the trail. It was the one in which John and the crew lived while the dam was being built, the one that so many people asked about while coming up the Northville-Lake Placid trail. The old root cellar is now completely overgrown, and would not be noticed by an unknowing hiker. Trees and under-growth have taken over the clearing, yielding only to the small path that is maintained through the middle of the "yard." The roots of the saplings reach into the old walls of the foundation, breaking them apart as they are turned back into dirt. It doesn't take long.

Heading west on the second day of my hike, I notice that the trails are not maintained as they were fourteen years ago. The grass and brush alongside the trails is a lot higher. Unfortunately, the trail crews are gone now, victims of state cut-backs and "budgetary restraints." The downed trees often sit in undisturbed silence for years, challenging the hikers to climb over, under, or around their outstretched limbs.

From the Beaver Pond on Cedar Lakes, I looked towards the south, attempting to view the tower on top of Pillsbury Mountain. I couldn't see any part of it. I believe that I'd have to be about another half-mile further north, as the view is blocked by the hills directly south of Cedar Lakes. From what I hear, the tower was only staffed for a short time after I left the area, and never reopened in 1982. The cabin is in rough shape, although the actual tower was purchased by a private company for commercial use.

The lean-to on Sampson Lake had been replaced as well, even though it was not very old or worn. The destruction of the earlier version had been sudden and complete. A violent windstorm during the summer of 1986 had dropped the massive "widowmaker" tree that had leaned precariously over the lean-to, reducing the log structure to a pile of splinters. It was only a stroke of luck that nobody had been in the lean-to on that particular night, as they never would have survived.

Reaching the site of John's old cabin on West Lake was not something that I had looked forward to. It was hard to swallow; the charred remains of the log building sitting quietly in the middle of the overgrown clearing. After many years of debate, the State had determined that all interior stations would be removed in order to comply with the wilderness land use regulations. And so, on a cold, snowy day in the winter of 1987, the cabin was intentionally torched, leaving behind only Adirondack Louie's fireplace to stand guard on the front lawn of West Lake. It was a lonely sight.

Barb Remias had sent me a photograph of the cabin being burned, with flames shooting out the doors and windows and towering over the solid shingled roof. I put the picture away as soon as it arrived, and never looked at it again. It was too hard to look at, and I'm certain that John had an equally difficult time giving the photo a second glance. It had been his home, and now it was gone.

By the time I made my return visit, John was gone, too. Suffering from a short illness, he passed away a couple of years before. I never got to say goodbye, which will always bother me. I stopped to reflect on the last words that John said to me those many years ago; about how the people would change, but the backcountry would remain the same. Looking at the sun over the hills on the far end of West Lake, I was amazed at how true his words had been, so many years before.

Sitting on the shore of West Lake in front of the remains of the old cabin, I could feel John's presence, in much the same way that I could sense the ghost of Adirondack French Louie strolling around the grounds.

I chuckled to myself, thinking about the possibility of John's ghost actually being there. And if he was there, would he still be the same old character, telling stories and perhaps trying to slip a few more rocks into my pack? I knew it was a ridiculous thought, and I tried brushing it aside. But finally, after a lengthy spell of quiet deliberation, I decided to unzip the various pockets and compartments of my pack, inspecting the contents for unfamiliar heavy objects before starting my walk back out of the woods. After all, John did have an active sense of humor, and he was extremely persistent. And I wasn't about to fall for the same trick a third time!

About the Author

Larry Weill's career life has been as diverse and interesting as the characters in his books. An avid naturalist and biologist, he studied biology and entomology prior to entering service as a wilderness ranger. A lifelong devotee to the mountains and "high places," he quickly fell in love with the tall peaks and grand scenery of the Adirondack Mountains.

Throughout his adult life, Larry has worked as a wilderness park ranger, a fire tower observer, a financial planner, a technical writer, and a career Navy Reservist. His unique and diverse resumé has provided him with a broad perspective on life, and given him a wonderful base from which his stories are told.

Throughout his experiences, he admits to a few constraints that have defined his life. An avid "people watcher," he enjoys observing and writing about people and their unique characteristics. These observations are an interesting thread that appears throughout his writings.

Larry's other passions include his family and the Adirondack Park. He lives in Rochester, New York, with his wife Patty and his two daughters, Kelly and Erin. They are frequent hikers and climbers in the Adirondack Mountains, and vacation there annually.